# Changing Me, Change the World

Presented To:

By:

On:

# Changing Me, Change *the* World

*Prayers from the Psalms,
Book One*

Lynnda Ell

WestBow Press

*WestBow Press™*
*1663 Liberty Drive*
*Bloomington, IN 47403*
*www.westbowpress.com*
*Phone: (866) 928-1240*

*© 2009 Lynnda Ell. All rights reserved.*

*No part of this book may be reproduced, stored in a retrieval system, or transmitted by any means without the written permission of the author.*

*First published by WestBow Press 12/15/2009*

*ISBN: 978-1-4497-0003-4 (sc)*
*ISBN: 978-1-4497-0004-1 (e)*
*ISBN: 978-1-4497-0005-8 (hc)*

*Library Congress of Control Number: 2009942832*

*Printed in the United States of America*
*Bloomington, Indiana*

*This book is printed on acid-free paper.*

*Scripture quotations are from The Holy Bible, English Standard Version® (ESV®), copyright © 2001 by Crossway, a publishing ministry of Good News Publishers. Used by permission. All rights reserved.*

To my mother, Muriel Watson

and in memory of my father,

John Eubanks

# Contents

| | |
|---|---|
| INTRODUCTION | 1 |
| PSALM 1 | 2 |
| CHOOSING THE WAY OF LIFE | 3 |
| PSALM 2 | 4 |
| WHY DO THE NATIONS CONSPIRE | 5 |
| PSALM 3 | 6 |
| I AM SUSTAINED | 7 |
| PSALM 4 | 8 |
| BREAKING THROUGH POWER STRUGGLES | 9 |
| PSALM 5 | 12 |
| YOU MAKE MY DAY | 13 |
| PSALM 6 | 16 |
| GRIEF WITH GREY HAIR | 17 |
| PSALM 7 | 18 |
| PSALM OF THE INNOCENT | 19 |
| PSALM 8 | 22 |
| PSALM OF THE NIGHT SKY | 23 |
| PSALM 9 | 24 |
| JUDGE OF THE NATIONS | 25 |
| PSALM 10 | 28 |
| PREDATORS OF THE POOR | 29 |

| | |
|---|---|
| PSALM 11 | 32 |
| *NOT* RUNNING AWAY | 33 |
| PSALM 12 | 34 |
| FALSE WORDS AND TRUE | 35 |
| PSALM 13 | 38 |
| FIFTY-SEVEN FOREVERS | 39 |
| PSALM 14 | 42 |
| EMPTY-HEADED FOOLS | 43 |
| PSALM 15 | 46 |
| MIRROR IMAGE | 47 |
| PSALM 16 | 48 |
| A BLESSING OF MY OWN | 49 |
| PSALM 17 | 52 |
| PRAYER OF THE PERSECUTED CHURCH | 53 |
| PSALM 18 | 56 |
| GREAT DELIVERANCE | 57 |
| PSALM 19 | 64 |
| THE *REAL* MESSAGE OF THE STARS | 65 |
| PSALM 20 | 68 |
| THE PRAYER OF BLESSING | 69 |
| PSALM 21 | 72 |
| GOD'S POWER TO BLESS, GOD'S STRENGTH TO DESTROY | 73 |
| PSALM 22 | 74 |

| | |
|---|---|
| CONTEMPLATION OF THE CRUCIFIXION OF CHRIST | 75 |
| PSALM 23 | 80 |
| THE BLESSINGS OF OBEDIENCE | 81 |
| PSALM 24 | 84 |
| THE EARTH FROM AGE TO AGE | 85 |
| PSALM 25 | 86 |
| WALKING BY FAITH | 87 |
| PSALM 26 | 90 |
| PROTECTION FROM HARMFUL CRITICISM | 91 |
| PSALM 27 | 92 |
| GETTING PAST FEAR | 93 |
| PSALM 28 | 96 |
| SMOOTH-TALKING OPERATORS | 97 |
| PSALM 29 | 98 |
| THE SONG OF THE THUNDERSTORM | 99 |
| PSALM 30 | 102 |
| I AM HEALED! | 103 |
| PSALM 31 | 104 |
| FORGIVENESS FOR SIN | 105 |
| PSALM 32 | 108 |
| REFLECTING ON FORGIVENESS | 109 |
| PSALM 33 | 112 |
| THE POWER OF GOD'S SPOKEN WORD | 113 |

| | |
|---|---|
| Psalm 34 | 116 |
| Freedom from Overwhelming Fear | 117 |
| Psalm 35 | 120 |
| Death by Gossip | 121 |
| Psalm 36 | 124 |
| The Desire to Destroy | 125 |
| Psalm 37 | 126 |
| Futile Fretting | 127 |
| Psalm 38 | 132 |
| Cry of Repentance | 133 |
| Psalm 39 | 136 |
| Open Mouth, Insert Foot | 137 |
| Psalm 40 | 140 |
| Gratitude for Deliverance | 141 |
| Psalm 41 | 144 |
| The Bedfast Psalm | 145 |

# Introduction

Answered prayer is a powerful force for change. I do not know why God chose to give us access to His power through prayer. From the time He created Adam and Eve, He gave us authority over the earth and told us to take care of it. He made us stewards of the earth with the responsibility of fulfilling His purpose. We lost that authority, and the power to use it, when we rebelled against God and ceased being His stewards. However, when God reconciled us to Himself by the sacrifice of Jesus on the cross, He restored that authority. As His redeemed children, we have power again to be His stewards. One of the ways we access that power is by praying.

An effective way to release God's power through prayer is to pray the words that He has given us in the Bible. We stand on a very firm foundation when we pray from the Bible. The writer of Hebrews says, "The word of God is… sharper than any two-edged sword." Praying scripture in agreement with God gives this weapon a delivery system. Prayer is the arm that wields the sword.

*Changing Me, Change the World* was written to encourage you to meditate on Psalms, the prayer-songs of the Bible, and to show you one way of praying them. Some of the prayers are deeply personal. Other prayers look past our needs and connect with other issues and other parts of God's kingdom. The prayers in this book are open-ended. That is, I did not end them with "Amen" or with "In Jesus' Name, Amen." This gives you the opportunity to continue praying in your own words as the Holy Spirit leads you.

Use these prayers as stepping-stones to greater intimacy with God. Read the Psalms and the prayers. Think about them. Pray them aloud. As you spend time with Him, the Holy Spirit will show you how to find your own words. He will guide you to pray for specific issues to accomplish His purpose. You will live an adventure unlike any you could have imagined. You will see God's will unfold on earth as it is in Heaven. How exciting is that?

Be blessed!

Lynnda Ell<br>
New Orleans, LA

# Psalm 1

1. Blessed is the man who walks not in the counsel of the wicked, nor stands in the way of sinners, nor sits in the seat of scoffers;

2. but his delight is in the law of the Lord, and on his law he meditates day and night.

3. He is like a tree planted by streams of water that yields its fruit in its season, and its leaf does not wither. In all that he does, he prospers.

4. The wicked are not so, but are like chaff that the wind drives away.

5. Therefore the wicked will not stand in the judgment, nor sinners in the congregation of the righteous;

6. for the Lord knows the way of the righteous, but the way of the wicked will perish.

# Choosing the Way of Life

Lord, I greatly desire this blessing; the blessing You give for *not* listening to the counsel of the ungodly.

"Follow us!" shout the commercials. "Buy this! Watch that! We know how you should live. Listen to us!" Everywhere I turn, advertisements demand my attention.

God, I *am* tempted. Many times the life they show sounds easy and fun. Sometimes I would like to "go there" and "buy that" and live a "carefree" life, especially when I am tired and my life seems more than I can handle.

Truly Lord, I want to follow only Your plans and purposes. Your Word shows me the eternal end of the ones who follow the counsel of the ungodly. I see the twisted lives of those who walk with sinners. I know the dark and empty thoughts of those who live as scornful mockers. No matter how beguiling the temptations of those who give ungodly counsel, You have shown me the truth behind the lies. I reject the counsel of the ungodly, the path of sinners and the seat of the scornful.

Lord, my delight is in You and my desire is in following Your law. I want to think about You and meditate on Your law night and day. Plant me firmly by Your streams of living water, so that I will bring forth fruit in Your seasons. Let me not wither, but prosper according to Your Word.

Father, let those who are wicked see that their lives are worthless without You. Show them that the end of their lives will be judgment and ruin. Let them seek a righteous life in You that lasts for eternity.

# Psalm 2

1 Why do the nations rage and the peoples plot in vain?

2 The kings of the earth set themselves, and the rulers take counsel together, against the Lord and against his anointed, saying,

3 "Let us burst their bonds apart and cast away their cords from us."

4 He who sits in the heavens laughs; the Lord holds them in derision.

5 Then he will speak to them in his wrath, and terrify them in his fury, saying,

6 "As for me, I have set my King on Zion, my holy hill."

7 I will tell of the decree: The Lord said to me, "You are my Son; today I have begotten you.

8 Ask of me, and I will make the nations your heritage, and the ends of the earth your possession.

9 You shall break them with a rod of iron and dash them in pieces like a potter's vessel."

10 Now therefore, O kings, be wise; be warned, O rulers of the earth.

11 Serve the Lord with fear, and rejoice with trembling.

12 Kiss the Son, lest he be angry, and you perish in the way, for his wrath is quickly kindled. Blessed are all who take refuge in him.

# Why Do the Nations Conspire

Lord, why do the nations conspire against You? Why do their citizens vainly imagine that they can dream up a scheme to escape Your control?

You know that our country is chief among the rebels. We choose leaders who do not know You. They take their places in the government and pass laws that ignore You. They disregard the consequences of their actions, and close their eyes to the effects these laws have upon Your people. Some of them purposely rebel against You. Others are indifferent to Your Way. The evil they release causes all of us to suffer.

Praise Your Name, Oh Lord! Regardless of the sinful ways of our leaders, You are in control. You must be much amused at their feeble attempts to forestall Your holy will and purpose. In scorn, You bring to their attention that there is only One True King. You have chosen Him and chosen His throne. You have crowned Your only begotten Son and placed him on Your holy hill of Zion.

Blessed is the Name of Jesus Christ, our Lord! You have given the nations as His inheritance and the uttermost parts of the world as His possession. He rules in hearts today. Yet the time is coming — and soon, Oh God — when You will send Your Son to rule the nations with a rod of iron. He will break the rebellion of the rulers as a potter breaks a badly shaped bowl.

Warn our leaders again, Lord. Teach them humility so that they may serve You with reverent awe and worshipful fear. Lead our rulers to honor Your Son, the King, before the judgment comes. Bless us as we take refuge in You and put our future in Your hands.

# Psalm 3

A Psalm of David, when he fled from Absalom his son.

1 O Lord, how many are my foes! Many are rising against me;

2 many are saying of my soul, there is no salvation for him in God.

*Selah*

3 But you, O Lord, are a shield about me, my glory, and the lifter of my head.

4 I cried aloud to the Lord, and he answered me from his holy hill.

*Selah*

5 I lay down and slept; I woke again, for the Lord sustained me.

6 I will not be afraid of many thousands of people who have set themselves against me all around.

7 Arise, O Lord! Save me, O my God! For you strike all my enemies on the cheek; you break the teeth of the wicked.

8 Salvation belongs to the Lord; your blessing be on your people!

*Selah*

# I Am Sustained

Father, David was distraught and afraid when his own son tried to kill him and take his throne away from him. My fear is a different kind. I do not have David's fear because I feel safe in Your hands. I know that no one can get to me unless You allow it. I fear for my country, though. I fear because so many of its citizens "rise up and trouble" me with the easy acceptance of lustful living and easy agreement to murder innocent babies. Many enemies rise up against the ideas of living lives of purity and of protecting the weak. They rise up because the values found in Your Word shine the light of truth upon these terrible sins and they reject Your way. Many are saying that they will change our country and that I will have no help from You.

But You, Oh Lord, are a shield about me, You are my glory and - in the midst of rebellion and ridicule - You are the lifter of my head. Praise Your Name, Oh Lord, because when I cry to You, You hear and answer.

Because I know that You hear me, I lie down and sleep, secure in the knowledge that You sustain me, whether I am awake or asleep. The knowledge that You sustain me amazes me, Lord. I am awed, humbled, grateful - I am sustained!

Meditating on that truth breaks through my fear. I am certain that You sustain me. You plant me firmly against the multitude that set themselves against Your Word. I will stand in faith while You "break the teeth of the ungodly."

My salvation comes from You, Oh Lord. You pour out both salvation and deliverance upon Your people. Even so, Lord, come to our defense.

# Psalm 4

1. Answer me when I call, O God of my righteousness! You have given me relief when I was in distress. Be gracious to me and hear my prayer!

2. O men, how long shall my honor be turned into shame? How long will you love vain words and seek after lies?

   *Selah*

3. But know that the Lord has set apart the godly for himself; the Lord hears when I call to him.

4. Be angry, and do not sin; ponder in your own hearts on your beds, and be silent.

   *Selah*

5. Offer right sacrifices, and put your trust in the Lord.

6. There are many who say, "Who will show us some good? Lift up the light of your face upon us, O Lord!"

7. You have put more joy in my heart than they have when their grain and wine abound.

8. In peace I will both lie down and sleep; for you alone, O Lord, make me dwell in safety.

# Breaking Through Power Struggles

Lord, I need Your presence in my life every second. More than air to breath, I need Your answers when I call out to You. Even when I do not call You, when my mind is too disturbed to make the call, I need You to "answer" me. Let Your care of me depend not on my reaching out to You but on Your great faithfulness.

I know that I can trust You to do this because so many times in my past when discord had me trapped, You set me free. Repeatedly, You have enlarged my ability to cope and to understand what is really happening when I was in distress. Have mercy on me when You hear my prayer, especially when I think You do not hear it.

Father, there are those around me who would turn my honor and dignity into shame. Sometimes, I am tempted to do the same to them. Forgive us all. Teach me to hate vanity, futility and seeking after position. Protect me from the power struggles at my job, in my family, and even at church. Protect me from participating in them and teach me to leave my honor and dignity in Your hands. Keep me from lashing out at people, because I could easily strike out at the wrong ones. I know, Oh Lord, that You have set me apart for Yourself and made me distinctly Yours. That is why I can trust You to protect me from internal politics. Thank You for that.

So Lord, when I feel slighted or overlooked in these power struggles, keep my anger and hurt feelings from causing me to sin. By the power of Your Spirit, let me take stock of my own heart and *not* say - or even think - things that would grieve You. Instead, I will give my anger and hurt feelings to You to purge so that You can restore Your joy and peace in my heart. I will trust You with my honor and my dignity. I will trust You for the outcome of all the power struggles. I will trust You with everything in my life.

# My Prayer

I will focus on You instead of focusing on the discord around me. Then I will see the light of Your countenance. That is the outcome I truly desire; then I have joy and rejoicing in my heart, regardless of the loss of things or the gain of position.

The light of Your countenance that allows me to sleep peacefully when I am troubled. You, alone, Lord, make me dwell in safety and You alone give me a confident trust.

Blessed be Your Name, Oh Lord!

# Psalm 5

1  Give ear to my words, O Lord; consider my groaning.

2  Give attention to the sound of my cry, my King and my God, for to you do I pray.

3  O Lord, in the morning you hear my voice; in the morning I prepare a sacrifice for you and watch.

4  For you are not a God who delights in wickedness; evil may not dwell with you.

5  The boastful shall not stand before your eyes; you hate all evildoers.

6  You destroy those who speak lies; the Lord abhors the bloodthirsty and deceitful man.

7  But I, through the abundance of your steadfast love, will enter your house. I will bow down toward your holy temple in the fear of you.

8  Lead me, O Lord, in your righteousness because of my enemies; make your way straight before me.

9  For there is no truth in their mouth; their inmost self is destruction; their throat is an open grave; they flatter with their tongue.

10  Make them bear their guilt, O God; let them fall by their own counsels; because of the abundance of their transgressions cast them out, for they have rebelled against you.

11  But let all who take refuge in you rejoice; let them ever sing for joy, and spread your protection over them, that those who love your name may exult in you.

12  For you bless the righteous, O Lord; you cover him with favor as with a shield.

# You Make My Day

Oh Lord, please hear my words, even when most of them are whiney and complaining. Just listen to my voice, for the words may not be very pretty. But Lord, in my times of self-pity, the truth is I have nowhere else to turn. Nor do I wish to come to anyone but You.

In the morning, You hear my voice. Sometimes I come rejoicing, grateful for waking with the feeling of good health and high energy, ready to share my joyful expectations with You. Sometimes I come to You filled with physical pain, having spent the night tossing and turning. Then my mental voice is harsh as I plead with You for the ability to deal with the pain. I try to get out of bed trusting You to get me through the pain to a place where I can be productive.

Sometimes I turn to You in the morning with my heart and mind filled with the needs of others. My petitions are on behalf of the friends, family, and co-workers who are a part of my life. But *always*, Lord, I come to you in the morning. For how could I start my day unless you are present? How could I cherish the day You give me unless You speak to my heart?

Keep me always sensitive to Your Spirit. I know that You are not a God who takes pleasure in wickedness. I do not take pleasure in wickedness either. I want to be like You. What I really want is to be a person who takes pleasure in You!

The evil person will not dwell even temporarily with You; an evil person is not given that privilege. You have given me the desire to live eternally in Your presence. Were it not for Jesus taking my punishment on the cross, You would exile me with the boasters, liars, bloodthirsty, and other people who do evil. Thank you for the honor – the gift – of living in Your presence.

# My Prayer

If I boast, let me boast only of Your mercy! I do not want to do evil, so purge the evil in my heart. I do not want to lie, so protect me from being a liar. I do not want to shed blood, instead give me courage to tell everyone how Jesus shed His blood for us!

As for me, I will enter into Your house and Your presence through the abundance of Your steadfast love and mercy. I will worship You in spirit and in truth. I will worship You in reverential respect and awe. As I worship You, Oh Lord, lead me into Your righteousness so that I do not fall into the traps of my enemies. Do not let me wander, but keep me on Your straight and level path.

I know that there is nothing trustworthy or truthful in my enemies' talk. Their hearts are destructive chasms. Their throats are like open sepulchers. Yet they are smooth-tongued flatterers who set me up for the fall. Show them their guilt, Oh Lord. When they reap what they sowed, bring them face to face with their need for repentance! If they do not repent, then cast them out because of their rebellious transgressions against You!

Lord, if my enemies repent, if they put their trust in You, then let them join me as I take refuge in You and rejoice in Your presence, for I was once like them.

Regardless of my enemies' response, I will sing and shout for joy because You are my covering and You defend me.

Hallelujah! Praise the Lord!

Let all those who love Your Name rejoice exceedingly. For You, Oh Lord, bless those to whom You have given right standing before You. Your pleasure and good favor shield those who trust in Jesus' Name. You make my day, every day. Blessed be the Name of the Lord!

# Psalm 6

1. O Lord, rebuke me not in your anger, nor discipline me in your wrath.

2. Be gracious to me, O Lord, for I am languishing; heal me, O Lord, for my bones are troubled.

3. My soul also is greatly troubled. But you, O Lord—how long?

4. Turn, O Lord, deliver my life; save me for the sake of your steadfast love.

5. For in death there is no remembrance of you; in Sheol who will give you praise?

6. I am weary with my moaning; every night I flood my bed with tears; I drench my couch with my weeping.

7. My eye wastes away because of grief; it grows weak because of all my foes.

8. Depart from me, all you workers of evil, for the Lord has heard the sound of my weeping.

9. The Lord has heard my plea; the Lord accepts my prayer.

10. All my enemies shall be ashamed and greatly troubled; they shall turn back and be put to shame in a moment.

# GRIEF WITH GREY HAIR

Father, there has never been a time when You rebuked or disciplined me that I did not deserve it. But please do not be angry with me. You know how weak I am. Right now, I feel completely isolated. Both my body and my mind are faint and withering away. Even my bones are troubled. Have mercy on me, Lord! Be gracious to me and heal me of this physical and mental anguish. Even my spirit is exceedingly disturbed and troubled. Father, I feel completely cut off from You.

How long, Oh Lord? How long is it until I feel Your presence and hear Your voice? Return to me and grant me swift relief. Save my life! Save me for the sake of your steadfast love and mercy.

Right now, I feel as far away from You as if I were dead. Right now, my woeful words of praise seem to go no higher than the ceiling. I groan so much, I weary myself. You must be fed up with my groaning, too. Yet I am not able to stop. Every night I soak my pillow with tears. In fact, I flood my whole bed. I am ruining my eyes with so much crying. It has gone on so long that even my grief has gray hair!

Yet the enemies of my soul stand around and gloat and I am sick of it. *Get out,* all of you evil ones! Get out and stay out! Why? Because *I know* my Lord has heard the voice of my weeping. *I know* my Lord has heard my supplications. *I know* my Lord receives my prayer. Even though I feel so all alone, my Lord will *not* desert me. I will *not* be ashamed and sorely troubled.

Lord, You trouble Your enemies, not me. I will *not* turn away from my Lord and be put to shame. Lord, You shame Your enemies, not me. As for me, I will wait upon my Lord. I trust my Lord, even when He is silent.

# Psalm 7

1 O Lord my God, in you do I take refuge; save me from all my pursuers and deliver me,

2 lest like a lion they tear my soul apart, rending it in pieces, with none to deliver.

3 O Lord my God, if I have done this, if there is wrong in my hands,

4 if I have repaid my friend with evil or plundered my enemy without cause,

5 let the enemy pursue my soul and overtake it, and let him trample my life to the ground and lay my glory in the dust.

*Selah*

6 Arise, O Lord, in your anger; lift yourself up against the fury of my enemies; awake for me; you have appointed a judgment.

7 Let the assembly of the peoples be gathered about you; over it return on high.

8 The Lord judges the peoples; judge me, O Lord, according to my righteousness and according to the integrity that is in me.

9 Oh, let the evil of the wicked come to an end, and may you establish the righteous—you who test the minds and hearts, O righteous God!

10 My shield is with God, who saves the upright in heart.

11 God is a righteous judge, and a God who feels indignation every day.

12 If a man does not repent, God will whet his sword; he has bent and readied his bow;

# Psalm of the Innocent

Help me, Lord! My enemies are pursuing and persecuting me unjustly. My enemies are trying to destroy me. Lord, You know that, this time, it is not my fault. If I have done anything my enemies say I have, let them catch me. Let them destroy my life and ruin my honor the way they are trying to do.

I have thought about this long and hard, Lord, and my conscience is clear. You be the judge. If I am innocent of their outrageous charges, then come to my defense. Protect me from their rage. Rise up and give me the justice and the vindication that You reserve for the innocent. Gather a group of my peers as a jury and You judge me. Then give me justice in accordance with my right standing with You and according to the integrity of my heart.

Lord, I know that You try men's hearts and minds and emotions. Is that what is happening now? Is this not enough? Will You not rid me of my wicked enemies? *You* are my *only* defense and shield. Save me! You are the righteous judge. Defend me!

I know how You work, Lord. If my enemies do not repent of their sins and turn to You, they become Your enemies. You will sharpen Your sword, string Your bow, and make ready fiery arrows to use against them.

Look at my enemies. They conceive iniquity, become pregnant with mischief, and give birth to lies! They have made a trap for me; if they do not repent, let them fall into their own trap. If they continue in rebellion to You, let their evil intentions and the violence they plan fall on their own heads.

Lord, I want to make peace with my enemies. When I see them change their evil ways, I will know it was You at work. You will hear me singing Your praises and telling everyone how You saved me from them, how You made them my brothers. Let it happen soon, Lord.

13 he has prepared for him his deadly weapons, making his arrows fiery shafts.

14 Behold, the wicked man conceives evil and is pregnant with mischief and gives birth to lies.

15 He makes a pit, digging it out, and falls into the hole that he has made.

16 His mischief returns upon his own head, and on his own skull his violence descends.

17 I will give to the Lord the thanks due to his righteousness, and I will sing praise to the name of the Lord, the Most High.

# My Prayer

# Psalm 8

1  O Lord, our Lord, how majestic is your name in all the earth! You have set your glory above the heavens.

2  Out of the mouth of babes and infants, you have established strength because of your foes, to still the enemy and the avenger.

3  When I look at your heavens, the work of your fingers, the moon and the stars, which you have set in place,

4  what is man that you are mindful of him, and the son of man that you care for him?

5  Yet you have made him a little lower than the heavenly beings and crowned him with glory and honor.

6  You have given him dominion over the works of your hands; you have put all things under his feet,

7  all sheep and oxen, and also the beasts of the field,

8  the birds of the heavens, and the fish of the sea, whatever passes along the paths of the seas.

9  O Lord, our Lord, how majestic is your name in all the earth!

# Psalm of the Night Sky

Oh Lord, my soul and spirit rise in exultant praise of Your glorious name!

Looking at the moon and the myriad of stars in Your night sky gives me the most awesome feeling. I feel like a baby - a tiny infant - that cannot understand its place in the universe. Yet look at the strength You give me every day to act on Your behalf. You silence Your enemies by giving me Your strength.

I look at all the wonders of the heavens that You created; I consider the orbits and paths through the universe that You have established. The majesty and grandeur of Your universe shows me how insignificant I am without You. I am so small and powerless against my own sinful nature that it is hard for me to understand why you pay any attention to me at all.

Yet look at the position that You created for us to fill. You gave us everything. You surrounded us with Your glory and honored us with Your friendship. You gave us authority over the works of Your hands. In fact, because of the relationship we have with You through Jesus, You have made us rulers over just about everything. As a down payment on that, we have authority over all the created beings on earth—domestic and wild animals, birds, and everything in the sea.

Sometimes thinking about Your purpose for us makes me feel proud – as if I had anything to do with it. Yet when I look into Your beautiful, majestic, glorious, night sky, the sight keeps my life in perspective. I remember that I might be one of those who have authority over all the earth, but You created all of this. The sight of the sky reminds me that anything of value that I am or have or do is possible *only* because of Your mercy. Oh Lord, my Lord, how majestic is Your name in all the earth!

# Psalm 9

1  I will give thanks to the Lord with my whole heart; I will recount all of your wonderful deeds.

2  I will be glad and exult in you; I will sing praise to your name, O Most High.

3  When my enemies turn back, they stumble and perish before your presence.

4  For you have maintained my just cause; you have sat on the throne, giving righteous judgment.

5  You have rebuked the nations; you have made the wicked perish; you have blotted out their name forever and ever.

6  The enemy came to an end in everlasting ruins; their cities you rooted out; the very memory of them has perished.

7  But the Lord sits enthroned forever; he has established his throne for justice,

8  and he judges the world with righteousness; he judges the peoples with uprightness.

9  The Lord is a stronghold for the oppressed, a stronghold in times of trouble.

10  And those who know your name put their trust in you, for you, O Lord, have not forsaken those who seek you.

11  Sing praises to the Lord, who sits enthroned in Zion! Tell among the peoples his deeds!

12  For he who avenges blood is mindful of them; he does not forget the cry of the afflicted.

13  Be gracious to me, O Lord! See my affliction from those who hate me, O you who lift me up from the gates of death,

# Judge of the Nations

Let me begin today, Lord, with praise to You. With my whole heart do I praise You. With the way I live my life, today, I will praise You. With my lips I will tell others of all Your marvelous works and wonderful deeds. Right now, I rejoice in You and look forward to a wonderful day. In my heart and with my spirit I sing praise to Your name. You are The Most High and my Lord.

I need especially to begin my day by praising You because it is a day of turmoil in the world. It is a very stressful time for our nation. I need to remember that in the past, Lord, when my enemies gathered around me, attacking me on all sides, You took care of me. You caused my enemies to perish before You. *You* maintained my cause. You were my righteous judge.

History shows me that You care for the nations in the same way. You have rebuked the nations and destroyed the wicked. Some nations have been so terrible that You have even blotted their names out of history. Around us, beneath our feet, are the ruins of nations and their cities that we know nothing about because You have picked them up and thrown them down, removing them from memory.

Lord, You were the Judge of the Nations in the past, You are the judge today, and You will be the judge in the future. I will not fear the present or the future for neither one can separate me from your love. Regardless of how the nations come and go, You have established Your throne of judgment and justice forever. Regardless of the restless evil, that forever seeks to control the world, You continue to minister justice to all the peoples of the world. You will *always* be a refuge and an impregnable stronghold in the times of trouble, - financial woes, social and international turmoil, times of destitution and despair.

Lord, I praise You because I can lean on You - as can all who calls upon Your name. I am well acquainted with Your mercy. We have been through some tough times in the past. Because we have, I know that

14 that I may recount all your praises, that in the gates of the daughter of Zion I may rejoice in your salvation.

15 The nations have sunk in the pit that they made; in the net that they hid their own foot has been caught.

16 The Lord has made himself known; he has executed judgment; the wicked are snared in the work of their own hands.

*Higgaion. Selah*

17 The wicked shall return to Sheol, all the nations that forget God.

18 For the needy shall not always be forgotten, and the hope of the poor shall not perish forever.

19 Arise, O Lord! Let not man prevail; let the nations be judged before you!

20 Put them in fear, O Lord! Let the nations know that they are but men!

*Selah*

I can confidently put my trust in You. I lean on You and call on Your name because You have *never* forsaken me.

I remember so many times when it seemed that the whole world was falling apart and You brought me through. I have been through fires and floods and not only survived, but also prospered. I look on my scars from those times and see them only as memorials to Your care. They give me reason to sing Your praise and opportunity to tell everyone that You are worthy of their trust in times of distress and dire need. You do not forget me when my own leaders betray me. You do not forget my cry in times of affliction.

Even as I remember Your past mercies, I ask for Your gracious mercy, again. The world is a dangerous place, and I feel threatened. Protect my life. Have mercy on me and give me a fresh reason to tell everyone how You have rescued me. Open my eyes so that I can recognize Your care of me, so that I can rejoice in Your salvation and in Your saving help.

Look at the nations, Lord. They are sinking down in the pit they dug. They trap themselves and others in the nets of lies they weave. They all rush headlong towards death because they forget You. For in their lies and in their rebellion against You, they ignore the needy ones in their land. They trample the meek. They steal from the poor.

Arise, Oh Lord! Let not these wicked leaders prevail! You are the sovereign judge of all the nations. Put them in fear of Your righteous judgment. Make them realize their frail nature. Show them how weak they truly are. Show the nations' leaders that they are only men.

Oh Lord, bring all this back to my mind during the day. Let me think about all this and confidently walk through whatever the day brings.

# Psalm 10

1 Why, O Lord, do you stand afar off? Why do you hide yourself in times of trouble?

2 In arrogance the wicked hotly pursue the poor; let them be caught in the schemes that they have devised.

3 For the wicked boasts of the desires of his soul, and the one greedy for gain curses and renounces the Lord.

4 In the pride of his face the wicked does not seek him; all his thoughts are, "There is no God."

5 His ways prosper at all times; your judgments are on high, out of his sight; as for all his foes, he puffs at them.

6 He says in his heart, "I shall not be moved; throughout all generations I shall not meet adversity."

7 His mouth is filled with cursing and deceit and oppression; under his tongue are mischief and iniquity.

8 He sits in ambush in the villages; in hiding places he murders the innocent. His eyes stealthily watch for the helpless;

9 he lurks in ambush like a lion in his thicket; he lurks that he may seize the poor; he seizes the poor when he draws him into his net.

10 The helpless are crushed, sink down, and fall by his might.

11 He says in his heart, "God has forgotten, he has hidden his face, he will never see it."

12 Arise, O Lord; O God, lift up your hand; forget not the afflicted.

13 Why does the wicked renounce God and say in his heart, "You will not call to account"?

# Predators of the Poor

Lord, sometimes I just do not understand Your plan. I know that You see the plight of the poor people in our city. I know You see all the work that Your children are doing to make their lives more bearable, because You are the One Who directs us to provide for some of their needs. What I do not understand is why You do not take a more active role in protecting them from evil men.

Con men, criminals, and some companies prey upon the poor. Why does it seem as if You distance Yourself from their plight? Why does it appear that You ignore the situation and let these predators throw them into ever-greater distress and desperation?

Lord, I know You see. These arrogant people take pride in chasing and hounding the poor. Why do You not act - give them a dose of their own medicine? Do You not see, Lord, that these wicked ones worship the greedy desires of their own hearts? They curse and renounce even the idea of You. In their arrogance, they actually believe that You do not even exist - so they certainly are not afraid of Your judgment. It looks like You give them a free rein to do whatever they want to the poor. They are always thinking up new ways to take what little money and goods the poor have. Then they turn them into their slaves, or cast them aside, destroyed! Lord, while they are doing this they think they are invincible, sneering at anyone who tries to stop them.

Do You know what they are thinking in their hearts, Lord? They are thinking, "We'll never be poor like our victims. We'll always have everything we want and so will our children."

Do You know what they are telling their victims, Lord? They speak lies, scams and false advertising, mischief, trouble and sin. Cursing, oppression and iniquity pour out of their mouths.

These wicked predators sit in ambush all over the city. They entice their prey into their traps over radio and TV. They hide in the dark corners

14 But you do see, for you note mischief and vexation, that you may take it into your hands; to you the helpless commits himself; you have been the helper of the fatherless.

15 Break the arm of the wicked and evildoer; call his wickedness to account till you find none.

16 The Lord is king forever and ever; the nations perish from his land.

17 O Lord, you hear the desire of the afflicted; you will strengthen their heart; you will incline your ear

18 to do justice to the fatherless and the oppressed, so that man who is of the earth may strike terror no more.

to slay the innocent. They stand on the street corners, watch for the poor, and seize what little they have right out of their hands.

Even in seemingly safe places, these people hide like hungry lions in a thicket, waiting to seize their prey. They spring their trap. They crush the poor. The poor sink down and they are helpless as mighty claws rip their lives apart.

What do these predators think about after they have satisfied their greedy appetites? They think, "We are so good! We can do this in the plain sight of everyone and no one will stop us."

Arise, Oh Lord! Get up and prove them wrong. Slap them down hard, Lord. Show these predators that You have not forgotten the helpless poor whom they have crushed.

Why do You let them think that they have nothing to fear for setting free their rapacious greed? Why have You not called them to account for their deeds? I know You see all this. I know that You record all this trouble and grief that the poor are having. I know that You are Helper of the Fatherless and protect the one who is committed to You. So show Your power, Lord! Break up the companies who rob from the poor. Destroy the con men's ability to deceive. Put the thieves, robbers, and murderers in prison so they cannot commit their evil deeds. Cause the mobs and drug rings and gangs to collapse. Search out all those who prey on the poor - wherever they can be found - and destroy their wickedness.

Lord, You are the King forever, regardless of the empty musings of these evil ones. All nations exist according to Your will. So act as our Righteous King. Hear the desire and the longing of the humble and the oppressed to be free of this evil.

Lord, not all of us are victims or victims-in-waiting. You have many children among the poor. Many of the poor follow You. Whether rich or poor, give all of us wisdom to escape the predators that surround us. Prepare, strengthen, and guide our hearts so that we can hear You showing us the way to safety.

Bring justice to the poor, the fatherless, and the oppressed so that no man - regardless of his schemes can terrify them any more.

# Psalm 11

1. In the Lord I take refuge; how can you say to my soul, "Flee like a bird to your mountain,

2. for behold, the wicked bend the bow; they have fitted their arrow to the string to shoot in the dark at the upright in heart;

3. if the foundations are destroyed, what can the righteous do?"

4. The Lord is in his holy temple; the Lord's throne is in heaven; his eyes see, his eyelids test, the children of man.

5. The Lord tests the righteous, but his soul hates the wicked and the one who loves violence.

6. Let him rain coals on the wicked; fire and sulfur and a scorching wind shall be the portion of their cup.

7. For the Lord is righteous; he loves righteous deeds; the upright shall behold his face.

# *NOT* Running Away

Lord, today I praise Your name because You are my refuge; I trust in You.

Sometimes I feel like running away from my life, but where would I go? Everywhere I look, I see the wicked waiting in ambush to shoot me. I can go no place on earth to escape from events I fear. Natural disasters wipe out cities. Across the world, societies collapse. In every nation, Your children are part of the suffering. What can we do? As I said—there is no escape.

In spite of this, I take comfort in one fact: *You* are in control! Your eyes see everything. Nothing happens outside of Your awareness. There is another lesson that You have taught me: You actively cause some things to happen in order to test the faith of Your children. That is one reason I know that trying to escape from the circumstances in my life is futile. I would only find the same kind of test waiting for me wherever I ran!

You have shown me the result of all the wicked ones who release evil upon the world. Because You abhor them, their end will come suddenly with violence. Fire, brimstone, and a deadly scorching wind will be their inheritance. I know this, Lord, because You are righteous and You will not allow them to escape. So, I will trust in You. I will stay right here without panic. I will obey Your Word. I will go through this time of testing. I will look forward to the day I see Your face. I will trust You.

# Psalm 12

1. Save, O Lord, for the godly one is gone; for the faithful have vanished from among the children of man.

2. Everyone utters lies to his neighbor; with flattering lips and a double heart they speak.

3. May the Lord cut off all flattering lips, the tongue that makes great boasts,

4. those who say, "With our tongue we will prevail, our lips are with us; who is master over us?"

5. "Because the poor are plundered, because the needy groan, I will now arise," says the Lord; "I will place him in the safety for which he longs."

6. The words of the Lord are pure words, like silver refined in a furnace on the ground, purified seven times.

7. You, O Lord, will keep them; you will guard us from this generation forever.

8. On every side the wicked prowl, as vileness is exalted among the children of man.

# False Words and True

Help, Lord!

I have been looking around our country, lately, and I am appalled to discover that principled and godly people seem to be disappearing. Faithfulness among Your people and the faithful of this new generation are hard to find.

How do I know? By listening to what our leaders are saying, by watching TV, by listening to the radio, and by talking to the people around me. I listen to the words that come out of my own mouth. I am ashamed.

Lord, what I hear is horrible and it is getting worse. Everywhere I listen, I hear cursing and curses, words of no use—worthless and empty of meaning.

What happened recently is a good example. One national leader confessed to making false statements, then denied that the admission was the same thing as admitting that he had lied! Lord, how can anyone "make false statements" without lying? Are not those empty and useless words?

Everywhere around me, I see lips speak flattering words only to learn in time that they are deceitful words spoken from a hypocritical heart. Recently, a national leader, a man, who professes Your name, gave very public counsel to another national leader over a matter of adultery. You expose the hidden sins, so the knowledge that he had fathered a child in his own adulterous relationship became public. There was no standard of purity here, only empty words and deceitful hearts. (How true are Your words; acts we do in secret You will expose to all.)

Father, will You not do something about this horrible situation? Change hearts, Lord!

# My Prayer

Work in those who live their lives speaking hollow words from deceitful hearts to come to You in sincere repentance. Show them the high road of pure speech from a clean heart. Lead them to a godly sorrow over their empty lives.

Nevertheless, Lord, if they reject Your call, cut off their flattering lips and the tongues that speak proud boasting. Cut down to size those who say, "I can say whatever I want—who will stop me? Certainly not God!"

Ah, Lord, but then I turn away from the world. I turn to the Bible and read *Your* words. What a difference!

"Now I will arise," You say, "because the poor are oppressed, because of the groans of the needy, I will protect them from those who malign them."

You are talking about me, Lord. I feel sorely oppressed by all the wickedness that I hear around me. My spirit groans because of the unrepented deceitfulness that seems to be everywhere. I long for the safety of being able to trust what other people say. I yearn for relief from deceitful leaders and for Your saving grace.

Can I trust what You say? Absolutely! Your words and promises are pure and true. They are as pure as precious metals that have been highly refined. You not only keep Your word, You remind me of Your promises if I forget them. So, Lord, I claim Your promise. I trust You to guard me and protect me from this evil generation that fills the air with wicked words and deceitful lies. It is a cause of shame that the society of which I am a part—my own world—exalts vileness and raises the most evil acts to the highest degree of praise. Father, see our sin, have mercy on us and save us.

# Psalm 13

1. How long, O Lord? Will you forget me forever? How long will you hide your face from me?

2. How long must I take counsel in my soul and have sorrow in my heart all the day? How long shall my enemy be exalted over me?

3. Consider and answer me, O Lord my God; light up my eyes, lest I sleep the sleep of death,

4. lest my enemy say, "I have prevailed over him," lest my foes rejoice because I am shaken.

5. But I have trusted in your steadfast love; my heart shall rejoice in your salvation.

6. I will sing to the Lord, because he has dealt bountifully with me.

# Fifty-Seven Forevers

Father? Are You there?

When I talk to You, it seems as if my prayers never make it to Your throne in Heaven. In fact, they do not get as far as the ceiling. I feel so cut off and alone. Have You forgotten me? How long will you leave me here - forgotten and alone? Forever? How long will I seek Your face only to have You hide it from me?

Everyday is exactly like the one before - full of cares and worries. I feel as if I am carrying the whole world on my shoulders—and no one even notices. Why am I unnoticed? Why do I never get a compliment? I just keep plodding along in this dreary place. If not for the work I do, nothing would be done – and nobody notices!

Will You listen to me, God? Will You do something about my situation? I am so depressed that I could die. Do something because I do not want my enemy to think he has won. I do not want the gossips to be glad because they hear I am having so much trouble.

I have already done all that I can do. I have trusted in You. I have leaned on Your mercy. I have confidently believed in Your loving kindness. Regardless of how sad or depressed I feel, I always turn to You. I remember the past. I remember other difficult times. Your love has been my salvation, and because You love me, I will see Your salvation with new eyes. You have caused my heart to rejoice, and because of Your presence in my life, I will rejoice, again.

Even though I don't really feel like doing it, I will sing songs of praise to You. My faith will cause my voice to rise in worship, regardless of the way I feel. While I am singing, I will remember the many times when You rescued me from my situation and from my emotions. When I looked up in the past, You always came to my aid. It is just that when I feel so badly time seems to stretch to all eternity and I think You are never going to reach me. Yet all the time I cannot see or hear You, You are reaching out to me; while I am bitterly complaining, You are patiently listening.

# My Prayer

I know Lord that it will not be long before Your peace replaces my depression. Shortly, I will see Your face, again. It is just that right now, Lord, that time seems like fifty-seven forevers away. Help, Lord!

# Psalm 14

1. The fool says in his heart, "There is no God." They are corrupt, they do abominable deeds, there is none who does good.

2. The Lord looks down from heaven on the children of man, to see if there are any who understand, who seek after God.

3. They have all turned aside; together they have become corrupt; there is none who does good, not even one.

4. Have they no knowledge, all the evildoers who eat up my people as they eat bread and do not call upon the Lord?

5. There they are in great terror, for God is with the generation of the righteous.

6. You would shame the plans of the poor, but the Lord is his refuge.

7. Oh, that salvation for Israel would come out of Zion! When the Lord restores the fortunes of his people, let Jacob rejoice, let Israel be glad.

# Empty-Headed Fools

Lord, have You taken a good look around here, lately? I have never seen more empty-headed fools around than I do today. They are corrupt. They do terrible things. In their self-centered egotism, they never consider doing what is good and right. They are who they are and they do what they do because they believe that You do not exist.

If You were to look down from Heaven and if You were to search for someone who understands Your truth, someone who uses that truth to deal wisely in everyday matters, and someone who seeks after You out of vital necessity, You would be looking for a needle in a haystack. Even people who consider themselves religious fail to meet Your standard. By Your Word, no one who comes to You without coming through Jesus can meet Your standard. The fools who reject the very idea of Your existence certainly have not bowed to Your Son as their Lord and Savior.

What are they thinking, Lord? They scornfully reject the thought that You provide *everything* for their personal existence. Even that is not enough. They go on to push out any influence in our society that You have through Your children. If they could, they would eat us for lunch!

You know, Lord, that does not even discourage me, because I know You. If these fools don't change their minds and mend their evil ways, You *will* deal with them. Moreover, before they get what they deserve, they will experience such a fear and a dread as cannot be described. You will pour out the fear that they have caused Your children - all at once - upon their own heads.

Yet You give us more good news. While these foolish ones are trying to shame us and to confound the plans You have given us to carry out, You will shelter and protect us from them. You are our safe refuge. Thank You, Lord! I do not have to be afraid. I can carry on patiently waiting for You to take care of the situation in Your perfect time.

# My Prayer

Oh, Lord, even as I carry out the work You have given me, I long for the day when You restore the fortunes of Your children. I look forward to the day when Jesus returns, bringing a heavenly host with him. I anticipate a wonderful time of celebration and rejoicing, of worshiping Jesus, my Lord and King. What a marvelous change from what I experience now in this foolish world.

Even so, Lord, come quickly!

# Psalm 15

1. O Lord, who shall sojourn in your tent? Who shall dwell on your holy hill?

2. He who walks blamelessly and does what is right and speaks truth in his heart;

3. who does not slander with his tongue and does no evil to his neighbor, nor takes up a reproach against his friend;

4. in whose eyes a vile person is despised, but who honors those who fear the Lord; who swears to his own hurt and does not change;

5. who does not put out his money at interest and does not take a bribe against the innocent. He who does these things shall never be moved.

# Mirror Image

Lord, when I look in the mirror, I do not always like the person looking back at me. I do not see the person I want to be or even the person other people think I am. I know whom it is that I want to see. I want to see a person who spends time talking to You and listening to You everyday. I want to be a person in whom Your Holy Spirit lives and who every day speaks words of truth. I want to live everyday according to Your standards, avoiding temptations and resisting evil.

I want to be a person who treats everyone with respect and fairness. I want to speak honestly and with kindness. I want to think the best of everyone, yet have Your truth planted so deeply in my heart that no one deceives me.

Lord, when I look into the mirror, I want to see a person who does not gossip. I want to see a person who neither hurts nor takes advantage of her friends. I want to see someone who is at peace with her neighbors.

Lord, behind those eyes looking back at me, I want to see a person who gives honor and respect to those You love, a person who does not idolize anyone for their wealth, power, or position in society. I want to see a person who respects herself enough to keep her promises though it costs her everything she has to do it.

Father, in that mirror, I want to see a good steward of the wealth that I have and of all my resources. I want to support generously both my physical and spiritual families. I want never to be ashamed to tell others where I get my money. I always want to know that I earned it honestly, with You as my source.

This, Father, would be the reflection of my *heart*. This is the person I will become as I walk on the path You set before me; then no matter what storm comes into my life, it will not destroy my integrity. My way of life and the fruit of my living will have made me the mirror image of Your Son.

# Psalm 16

1  Preserve me, O God, for in you I take refuge.

2  I say to the Lord, "You are my Lord; I have no good apart from you."

3  As for the saints in the land, they are the excellent ones, in whom is all my delight.

4  The sorrows of those who run after another god shall multiply; their drink offerings of blood I will not pour out or take their names on my lips.

5  The Lord is my chosen portion and my cup; you hold my lot.

6  The lines have fallen for me in pleasant places; indeed, I have a beautiful inheritance.

7  I bless the Lord who gives me counsel; in the night also my heart instructs me.

8  I have set the Lord always before me; because he is at my right hand, I shall not be shaken.

9  Therefore my heart is glad, and my whole being rejoices; my flesh also dwells secure.

10  For you will not abandon my soul to Sheol, or let your holy one see corruption.

11  You make known to me the path of life; in your presence there is fullness of joy; at your right hand are pleasures forevermore.

# A Blessing of My Own

God, does anyone else have such a wonderful life as I have? If so, I cannot imagine it. Here I am, totally protected and guarded by You. Nothing can get to me that has not come past You first. Moreover, You prepare me to face whatever is to come in the future. You are always my wall of protection from the outside world and my refuge from daily trials.

I look at the person that I might have been, at the things I might have done. Without Your intervention, what a shameful life I might be leading. Instead, You invited me to be part of Your family and I accepted, changing my life forever. That day, You became my God. I absolutely know that without You being in my heart, I have nothing good inside of me.

You changed my friends, too. Some of them went away because they did not like the new me, but others wanted the same changes in their lives. That is a good thing, Lord, because now I am happiest when I am around other people who have You as God in their lives, too. I delight in their friendship and in the opportunities to share with them the adventures we have because You are in our lives. I look at others that I might have called my friends - people who have made power or wealth or social position or lust or evil or hatred their god. I see how empty their lives are, or jaded. I am appalled and grieved. Part of that feeling comes from the knowledge that I could easily have gone the same way if not for Your love and grace and mercy. Instead, You chose me, and I chose You. Now You hold and maintain my lot in life. Oh, how marvelously You have set me in pleasant places! Even my family - godly parents and loving children - are gifts from You.

How I thank and praise You, Lord. Every day You show me how to walk. Even in my dreams at night, You instruct me. I have no fear of nightmares because You are there even in my dreams. I have set You continually before me, day and night.

# My Prayer

Without You, I would be totally without protection. With You as my shield, fiercely raging storms shall not move me. I am always protected in the eye of the hurricane. The winds of adversity never touch my soul. Therefore, my heart is glad and my spirit rejoices. Even my body is at rest, removed from everyday stress and anxiety. I confidently dwell in safety wherever You lead me.

Even when my earthly life is over, You will not abandon me. Instead, You will lead me to a richer life in Your presence. In Your presence, I will experience a fullness of joy that I only glimpse in this life. You are preparing me for unimaginable pleasures for eternity.

God, has anyone ever been blessed such as I?

# Psalm 17

1 Hear a just cause, O Lord; attend to my cry! Give ear to my prayer from lips free of deceit!

2 From your presence let my vindication come! Let your eyes behold the right!

3 You have tried my heart, you have visited me by night, you have tested me, and you will find nothing; I have purposed that my mouth will not transgress.

4 With regard to the works of man, by the word of your lips I have avoided the ways of the violent.

5 My steps have held fast to your paths; my feet have not slipped.

6 I call upon you, for you will answer me, O God; incline your ear to me; hear my words.

7 Wondrously show your steadfast love, O Savior of those who seek refuge from their adversaries at your right hand.

8 Keep me as the apple of your eye; hide me in the shadow of your wings,

9 from the wicked who do me violence, my deadly enemies who surround me.

10 They close their hearts to pity; with their mouths they speak arrogantly.

11 They have now surrounded our steps; they set their eyes to cast us to the ground.

12 He is like a lion eager to tear, as a young lion lurking in ambush.

13 Arise, O Lord! Confront him, subdue him! Deliver my soul from the wicked by your sword,

# Prayer of the Persecuted Church

Father, Your children are calling. Hear our fearful, piercing cries of pain and despair. Give ear to our heartfelt and desperate prayers. Only You can vindicate us, Lord. Only You can turn our persecution into justice and peace.

You have proven our hearts, Lord. You have visited us in the night of our imprisonment. You have tested us as they took away our families. You have found no evil purpose in Your people. Instead, You have seen your children refuse to deny and curse You, in spite of all our loss and pain - even to the death of those we love.

Do You see Your church becoming violent? No! Instead, we are obeying Your Word, walking in the path to which You have called us. Our feet have not slipped from the Way.

Now we are calling on You, Oh God, for You will hear us. Incline Your ear to us and hear our prayer. Show Your marvelous loving kindness to Your persecuted church, Oh God. You who save by Your right hand protect those who trust and take refuge in You. Save us from those who rise up against us. Keep and guard us as the apple of Your eye. Hide us in the shadow of Your wings from the wicked that despoil and oppress us. Save us from the deadly adversaries who surround us.

Our adversaries think that their position and prosperity keeps them safe from judgment. They have hardened their hearts against Your people. They make exorbitant claims and arrogantly speak about wiping out Your influence and will.

Even when we go into hiding to protect ourselves, our enemies track us down. They surround us and, filled with evil intent, destroy us all, male and female, young and old. They take pity on no one. They are like lions savagely and eagerly tearing their prey.

Arise, Oh Lord! Confront and forestall these evil men. Cast them down! Deliver us from the wicked by Your sword. From men - by Your

**14** from men by your hand, O Lord, from men of the world whose portion is in this life. You fill their womb with treasure; they are satisfied with children, and they leave their abundance to their infants.

**15** As for me, I shall behold your face in righteousness; when I awake, I shall be satisfied with your likeness.

hand, Oh Lord - from men of the world who choose to persecute and to steal, save us, Oh Lord.

They fill their bellies with the wealth You provided for us. Their children are satiated on the blood of the slain. They give the remnants to their babies as toys.

As for Your children, Your church, we shall continue looking upon Your face by faith. We shall stand, even when our backs are beaten. Even to our deaths, we will remain faithful.

We shall be satisfied when we awake face to face with You and when we rest in sweet communion with You.

# Psalm 18

A Psalm of David, the servant of the Lord, who addressed the words of this song to the Lord on the day when the Lord rescued him from the hand of all his enemies, and from the hand of Saul. He said:

1. I love you, O Lord, my strength.

2. The Lord is my rock and my fortress and my deliverer, my God, my rock, in whom I take refuge, my shield, and the horn of my salvation, my stronghold.

3. I call upon the Lord, who is worthy to be praised, and I am saved from my enemies.

4. The cords of death encompassed me; the torrents of destruction assailed me;

5. the cords of Sheol entangled me; the snares of death confronted me.

6. In my distress I called upon the Lord; to my God I cried for help. From his temple he heard my voice, and my cry to him reached his ears.

7. Then the earth reeled and rocked; the foundations also of the mountains trembled and quaked, because he was angry.

8. Smoke went up from his nostrils, and devouring fire from his mouth; glowing coals flamed forth from him.

9. He bowed the heavens and came down; thick darkness was under his feet.

10. He rode on a cherub and flew; he came swiftly on the wings of the wind.

11. He made darkness his covering, his canopy around him, thick clouds dark with water.

# GREAT DELIVERANCE

Lord, I love You with everything inside of me.

In every way, I recognize that I would be nothing, that I would do nothing, and that I would have nothing, without You. You are my every strength – physical, mental, emotional, and spiritual. You are the Rock, the foundation of my life. When I feel weak and tired, You are the fortress where I can go to rest in safety. You are my God, so when my enemy attacks me, I come to You for refuge. I come to You for salvation from my enemies. I come to You for guidance and protection while I continue to fight the battles. All of this You give me when I call on You. My enemies do not stand a chance.

I have been near death before - it was a scary thing. You heard my prayers and moved Heaven and earth to bring me back. You delivered me from my strong enemy and from those who hated and abhorred me, for they were too strong for me. You were my anchor and support. You brought me into a large place, safe from traps and ambushes. You delivered me because You were pleased with me and because You delighted in me.

For my whole life, Lord, You have rewarded me - not according to any mighty works or acts of piety, but according to my steadfast integrity and sincerity with You. I have reaped what I have sown - whether good or bad, but I have tried to sow only good seed, keeping Your ways and living in obedience. I have always loved Your Word and tried to obey what I understand. You know my failures and You know my heart. Keep me pure and undefiled before You because of the sacrifice of Your Son.

I know how You work. You make people's lives a true reflection of the person they are inside themselves. With those who are kind and merciful, You show Yourself as kind and merciful. With an upright man, You show Yourself upright. With the pure, You show Yourself pure, and with the perverse, You show Yourself contrary. For you deliver people who are humble and afflicted, but you bring down those who are arrogant.

12 Out of the brightness before him hailstones and coals of fire broke through his clouds.

13 The Lord also thundered in the heavens, and the Most High uttered his voice, hailstones and coals of fire.

14 And he sent out his arrows and scattered them; he flashed forth lightnings and routed them.

15 Then the channels of the sea were seen, and the foundations of the world were laid bare at your rebuke, O Lord, at the blast of the breath of your nostrils.

16 He sent from on high, he took me; he drew me out of many waters.

17 He rescued me from my strong enemy and from those who hated me, for they were too mighty for me.

18 They confronted me in the day of my calamity, but the Lord was my support.

19 He brought me out into a broad place; he rescued me, because he delighted in me.

20 The Lord dealt with me according to my righteousness; according to the cleanness of my hands he rewarded me.

21 For I have kept the ways of the Lord, and have not wickedly departed from my God.

22 For all his rules were before me, and his statutes I did not put away from me.

23 I was blameless before him, and I kept myself from my guilt.

24 So the Lord has rewarded me according to my righteousness, according to the cleanness of my hands in his sight.

25 With the merciful you show yourself merciful; with the blameless man you show yourself blameless;

You are my light. In fact - You light up my whole life! Every step of the way, I see the direction I am going because You light the way.

Of course, the path is not always smooth and peaceful, so You have also given me the strength to plow through opposition and the power to leap over obstacles, if You have not removed the obstacle before I even knew it was there, which You often do.

You know, Lord, that this is not just some theoretical observation. You and I have been through some very trying times. You have never let me down. Through fire or flood, You have always been my Rock. You have tested me on some dangerously high places, but You set my feet so securely that I could stand firmly and not fall. Through trials, trouble, or testing, I can always trust You.

I am grateful that many times You prepare me in advance for the next stage in my life. I am never entirely sure just which set of circumstances in this part of my life is training for the next phase. That makes each day's activities more interesting. It takes away the worry that I will not be ready for the future. It makes the transition from one phase to the next so much easier for me because I know that You have everything under control. It keeps me from stumbling as I move into the next stage. Thank You for understanding that I need Your gentle and considerate care.

Sometimes, the phase of life that I am stepping into is spiritual warfare. I am especially grateful for the advance training, then. With it, I can face the battle with confidence, knowing that You are going before me - strengthening my arm, deflecting the enemies' weapons, and scattering the enemies before me.

Lord, You deliver me from Satan and all my enemies. You lift me up above those who rise up against me. Thank You, Lord, for all the times You have done this. I sing Your praises and tell everyone I know that You are the only reason I am still alive.

Great are Your deliverances and triumphs that You give to me. You show me Your mercy and steadfast love every day.

Blessed be the name of the Lord!

26 with the purified you show yourself pure; and with the crooked you make yourself seem tortuous.

27 For you save a humble people, but the haughty eyes you bring down.

28 For it is you who light my lamp; the Lord my God lightens my darkness.

29 For by you I can run against a troop, and by my God I can leap over a wall.

30 This God—his way is perfect; the word of the Lord proves true; he is a shield for all those who take refuge in him.

31 For who is God, but the Lord? And who is a rock, except our God?—

32 the God who I equipped me with strength and made my way blameless.

33 He made my feet like the feet of a deer and set me secure on the heights.

34 He trains my hands for war, so that my arms can bend a bow of bronze.

35 You have given me the shield of your salvation, and your right hand supported me, and your gentleness made me great.

36 You gave a wide place for my steps under me, and my feet did not slip.

37 I pursued my enemies and overtook them, and did not turn back till they were consumed.

38 I thrust them through, so that they were not able to rise; they fell under my feet.

39 For you equipped me with strength for the battle; you made those who rise against me sink under me.

# MY PRAYER

40 You made my enemies turn their backs to me, and those who hated me I destroyed.

41 They cried for help, but there was none to save; they cried to the Lord, but he did not answer them.

42 I beat them fine as dust before the wind; I cast them out like the mire of the streets.

43 You delivered me from strife with the people; you made me the head of the nations; people whom I had not known served me.

44 As soon as they heard of me they obeyed me; foreigners came cringing to me.

45 Foreigners lost heart and came trembling out of their fortresses.

46 The Lord lives, and blessed be my rock, and exalted be the God of my salvation—

47 the God who gave me vengeance and subdued peoples under me,

48 who delivered me from my enemies; yes, you exalted me above those who rose against me; you rescued me from the man of violence.

49 For this I will praise you, O Lord, among the nations, and sing to your name.

50 Great salvation he brings to his king, and shows steadfast love to his anointed, to David and his offspring forever.

# My Prayer

# Psalm 19

1 The Heavens declare the glory of God, and the sky above proclaims his handiwork.

2 Day to day pours out speech, and night to night reveals knowledge.

3 There is no speech, nor are there words, whose voice is not heard.

4 Their measuring line goes out through all the earth, and their words to the end of the world. In them he has set a tent for the sun,

5 which comes out like a bridegroom leaving his chamber, and, like a strong man, runs its course with joy.

6 Its rising is from the end of the heavens, and its circuit to the end of them, and there is nothing hidden from its heat.

7 The law of the Lord is perfect, reviving the soul; the testimony of the Lord is sure, making wise the simple;

8 the precepts of the Lord are right, rejoicing the heart; the commandment of the Lord is pure, enlightening the eyes;

9 the fear of the Lord is clean, enduring forever; the rules of the Lord are true, and righteous altogether.

10 More to be desired are they than gold, even much fine gold; sweeter also than honey and drippings of the honeycomb.

11 Moreover, by them is your servant warned; in keeping them there is great reward.

12 Who can discern his errors? Declare me innocent from hidden faults.

13 Keep back your servant also from presumptuous sins; let them not have dominion over me! Then I shall be blameless, and innocent of great transgression.

14 Let the words of my mouth and the meditation of my heart be acceptable in your sight, O Lord, my rock and my redeemer.

# The *Real* Message of the Stars

The Heaven declares Your glory, Oh Lord, and the sky - all the way to the most distant stars - declares Your handiwork.

Down here on earth, men pour out empty speech from a thousand languages day after day. Night after night, they talk to show how smart they are and to prove how much they know.

There is no speech from the stars and no voice to speak a word. Nonetheless, their "voices" are heard all over the world. The sun "speaks" every day. In the morning, it rises as cheerfully as a bridegroom does on his wedding day. It rejoices like a strong man at the beginning of a marathon. If none can hear what the distant stars are saying, they cannot avoid the voice of the sun.

What are these stars saying, Lord? They are telling the whole world about You. They are saying that Your law is perfect, restoring health to the whole person. Your every word is Truth, making wise the simple. Your laws are right, causing our hearts to rejoice. Your commands are pure and bright, enlightening our eyes even more than sunlight. A reverent, holy fear of You brings us to eternal life. Your decrees are altogether true and righteous.

If only we would spend less time listening to our own idle speech and more time paying attention to what the stars are saying! If only everyone would listen to their message. Then we would see that Your laws, precepts, and decrees are more desirable than all the purest gold in the world. We would see that Your Words are sweeter than the honey in the honeycomb.

If we would stop our incessant babbling long enough to listen, we would find out what the stars already know. We would learn that in keeping Your Word, we would have great reward. Your Word warns, reminds, illuminates and instructs Your servants.

# My Prayer

Father, let me be still before You and listen to the message of the stars. Show me my lapses and my errors. Clear from me my hidden faults. Keep me from presumptuous sins. Protect me from committing great transgressions. Keep me listening to and obeying Your Word.

Lord, when it is finally time for me to speak, let my voice be as faithful to You as the voice of the stars. Let every single word that I speak and every thought and purpose in my heart be pleasing to You and reflect Your glory. You, Oh Lord, are my Rock and my Redeemer and I desire to proclaim it with my life in the magnificent way the heavens declare Your glory.

# Psalm 20

1 May the Lord answer you in the day of trouble! May the name of the God of Jacob protect you!

2 May he send you help from the sanctuary and give you support from Zion!

3 May he remember all your offerings and regard with favor your burnt sacrifices!

*Selah*

4 May he grant you your heart's desire and fulfill all your plans!

5 May we shout for joy over your salvation, and in the name of our God set up our banners! May the Lord fulfill all your petitions!

6 Now I know that the Lord saves his anointed; he will answer him from his holy heaven with the saving might of his right hand.

7 Some trust in chariots and some in horses, but we trust in the name of the Lord our God.

8 They collapse and fall, but we rise and stand upright.

9 O Lord, save the king! May he answer us when we call.

# The Prayer of Blessing

Lord, I really do not know how to begin this prayer. Your Word contains such a wonderful blessing that I want to claim for everyone in my life. I want to bless my Mother, my daughters, my sons-in-law and my grandchildren with it. I want to speak it again over the pastors that You have given to our church. I want to pray it for the governor of our state and the president of our country. I want to claim it for Your children all over the world who are in pain or in danger or in despair.

Therefore, Lord, in Your presence, I speak this blessing:

In the Name of Jesus

"May the Lord answer you in the day of trouble.

May the Name of the God of Jacob set you up on a high place out of your enemies' reach and defend you.

May He send you help from His Sanctuary and strengthen you from Zion.

May He remember all your offerings and accept your sacrifice of praise.

May He grant you according to your heart's desire and fulfill all your plans.

May the Lord fulfill all your requests.

May we celebrate together in triumph at your salvation and victory and in the Name of our God may we publish it abroad to His glory."

# My Prayer

Lord, this is my prayer for everyone in my life and for all those whom You have chosen to receive it. I know that You hear my prayer, that You will save Your anointed and that You will answer from Your holy heaven with the strength of Your right hand. While some trust in other people or things for their safety, Your children will trust in Your Name. The others all eventually fall, but we stand upright before You.

Oh Lord, release this blessing from heaven. Let our Savior and King answer us when we call.

# Psalm 21

1 O Lord, in your strength the king rejoices, and in your salvation how greatly he exults!

2 You have given him his heart's desire and have not withheld the request of his lips.

*Selah*

3 For you meet him with rich blessings; you set a crown of fine gold upon his head.

4 He asked life of you; you gave it to him, length of days forever and ever.

5 His glory is great through your salvation; splendor and majesty you bestow on him.

6 For you make him most blessed forever; you make him glad with the joy of your presence.

7 For the king trusts in the Lord, and through the steadfast love of the Most High he shall not be moved.

8 Your hand will find out all your enemies; your right hand will find out those who hate you.

9 You will make them as a blazing oven when you appear. The Lord will swallow them up in his wrath, and fire will consume them.

10 You will destroy their descendants from the earth, and their offspring from among the children of man.

11 Though they plan evil against you, though they devise mischief, they will not succeed.

12 For you will put them to flight; you will aim at their faces with your bows.

13 Be exalted, O Lord, in your strength! We will sing and praise your power.

# God's Power to Bless, God's Strength to Destroy

I rejoice in Your strength, Oh Lord. In Your salvation, how greatly I rejoice! You have given me my heart's desire and not withheld the requests of my lips. Just thinking about that brings me to my knees in worship, Lord.

You send an abundance of good things to meet me. You set a crown of pure gold on my head as a royal daughter adopted into Your family. I asked You for life and You gave it to me, eternal life, lived in Your presence is mine. How awesome is *that*?

Lord, I trust You, rely on You, and place my confidence in You. I know, without a doubt, that because of Your mercy and steadfast love for me, nothing shall move me.

Your right hand shall find all Your enemies. Your right hand shall find all those who hate You. You will make them ignite in the time of Your anger. You will swallow them up in Your wrath and the fire will utterly consume them. You will destroy them from the earth, and their sons from among the children of men. For they plan evil against You. They conceive a cunning plot that will collapse into ruin. For You will distract them, making them turn their attention towards You. You will force them to face You, their divine judge.

Be exalted, Oh Lord, for who You are and for what You are doing. I will sing and I will praise You for Your unlimited power!

# Psalm 22

1. My God, my God, why have you forsaken me? Why are you so far from saving me, from the words of my groaning?

2. O my God, I cry by day, but you do not answer, and by night, but I find no rest.

3. Yet you are holy, enthroned on the praises of Israel.

4. In you our fathers trusted; they trusted, and you delivered them.

5. To you they cried and were rescued; in you they trusted and were not put to shame.

6. But I am a worm and not a man, scorned by mankind and despised by the people.

7. All who see me mock me; they make mouths at me; they wag their heads;

8. "He trusts in the Lord; let him deliver him; let him rescue him, for he delights in him!"

9. Yet you are he who took me from the womb; you made me trust you at my mother's breasts.

10. On you was I cast from my birth, and from my mother's womb you have been my God.

11. Be not far from me, for trouble is near, and there is none to help.

12. Many bulls encompass me; strong bulls of Bashan surround me;

13. they open wide their mouths at me, like a ravening and roaring lion.

14. I am poured out like water, and all my bones are out of joint; my heart is like wax; it is melted within my breast;

# Contemplation of the Crucifixion of Christ

God, why did You forsake Him? Until that moment came, He was totally united with You. The very thing that we humans hold most lightly—sweet communion with You—is the thing that Christ valued as much as life itself. Jesus willingly gave up His equality with You to become Your only begotten Son on earth. He knew that once on earth He would give up His life as the pure, sinless lamb, sacrificed for us all. Did He *know* how it would feel when You left Him all alone at the very point of His most appalling need for You? Yes, I guess He did. He sweat drops of blood in the garden when He asked You if it was necessary.

Bud how *could* You, God? How could You love me so much that You could conspire together to forsake – even for a moment - the sweet unity You shared?

Christ's defining moment as a human being was that period of separation. Only at the completion of His crucifixion was He a man all alone in His own skin. You were "far from helping" Him with Your power. You, who shared His every thought before it became words, was now "far from the words of His groaning."

During the day and the night before His crucifixion, did He cry out to You for release from this duty as He did in the Garden? Was the horror of the event pressing in on Him even as He faced the mock trials? I cannot really know the answer to that. I do know that Jesus never lost His confidence in You. He trusted You to deliver Him. He knew that You would not disappoint Him. He needed that faith and confidence in You when they scorned Him and heaped their hatred upon His head.

Once they had Him hanging on the cross, they laughed at Him and mocked Him saying, "This Man trusted that The Lord would deliver him - so let the Lord deliver Him, seeing that God delights in Him so much!"

15 my strength is dried up like a potsherd, and my tongue sticks to my jaws; you lay me in the dust of death.

16 For dogs encompass me; a company of evildoers encircles me; they have pierced my hands and feet—

17 I can count all my bones—they stare and gloat over me;

18 they divide my garments among them, and for my clothing they cast lots.

19 But you, O Lord, do not be far off! O you my help, come quickly to my aid!

20 Deliver my soul from the sword, my precious life from the power of the dog!

21 Save me from the mouth of the lion! You have rescued me from the horns of the wild oxen!

22 I will tell of your name to my brothers; in the midst of the congregation I will praise you:

23 You who fear the Lord, praise him! All you offspring of Jacob, glorify him, and stand in awe of him, all you offspring of Israel!

24 For he has not despised or abhorred the affliction of the afflicted, and he has not hidden his face from him, but has heard, when he cried to him.

25 From you comes my praise in the great congregation; my vows I will perform before those who fear him.

26 The afflicted shall eat and be satisfied; those who seek him shall praise the Lord! May your hearts live forever!

27 All the ends of the earth shall remember and turn to the Lord, and all the families of the nations shall worship before you.

28 For kingship belongs to the Lord, and he rules over the nations.

What did Jesus do in response? He reminded Himself that He had been born for this purpose. What was His one crying desire? It was not to come down from the cross – no! - He just wanted You to stay with Him, for the time to bear the world's sins to the death was coming and there was no one to help Him through it.

Already His enemies had surrounded Him and buried Him under their hatred. Already His body was dying: bones out of joint, heart failing, great manly strength dried up and tissues dehydrated. They had even stripped Him naked and gambled for possession of His clothes.

While all of this was going on, what was His heart cry to You? "Be not far from me, Oh Lord, Oh my Help!"

One last time He asked You to deliver Him from that moment of abandonment. He dreaded separation from You so much that He fought against it to the very end.

Then, Oh Lord, the most amazing thing happened. He looked beyond that moment. He took His eyes off what He dreaded. Instead, He looked at the effect of His obedience to You. Even though He had no illusions about how horrible "sinful aloneness" would be, *He stopped looking at it!* Instead, He saw Himself praising You while standing with all the people who could be there only because of His sacrifice. He saw that His separation from You was the One Answer for all of humanity who cried out in their sinful condition. He saw the poor and the afflicted with new hearts and satisfying relationships with You. He saw Your children worshiping You in Spirit and in Truth. He saw Himself honored as the Ruler of the Nations. He saw all the people who would accept His sacrifice serving You. He saw the world confessing that it was all because "He had done it."

Finally, He saw that because He was separated from You at His crucifixion, that the Great Separation was over. Your punishment for humanity's rebellion was poured out forever for those who would accept it. The Way is clear, now, for us to come to You.

Therefore, He endured, Father, therefore He endured.

**29** All the prosperous of the earth eat and worship; before him shall bow all who go down to the dust, even the one who could not keep himself alive.

**30** Posterity shall serve him; it shall be told of the Lord to the coming generation;

**31** they shall come and proclaim his righteousness to a people yet unborn, that he has done it.

# My Prayer

# Psalm 23

1. The Lord is my shepherd; I shall not want.

2. He makes me lie down in green pastures. He leads me beside still waters.

3. He restores my soul. He leads me in paths of righteousness for his name's sake.

4. Even though I walk through the valley of the shadow of death, I will fear no evil, for you are with me; your rod and your staff, they comfort me.

5. You prepare a table before me in the presence of my enemies; you anoint my head with oil; my cup overflows.

6. Surely goodness and mercy shall follow me all the days of my life, and I shall dwell in the house of the Lord forever.

# The Blessings of Obedience

Lord, I do not know how to be a good sheep. Having a "flock" of people like me would be a lot like having a gaggle of cats to herd - self-willed, independent, and opinionated! I know it takes all your love and abundant patience to be my shepherd and to teach me to follow.

I recall one lesson that took me 19 years to learn with You nudging me and coaching me all the way. You tried to feed me. You tried to guide me. You tried to shield me. For 19 years, I insisted on staying in the rocky, barren, arid wasteland. When (finally) I went in the direction You were leading, I ended up resting in the green pastures. (After fighting for 19 years to have my own way I was exhausted and needed to rest!)

When I followed You, You led me beside the pure river of living water where I found refreshment and peace. Why did I fight You so long?

Once I had decided that it was more important to obey You than to have my own way, I could not understand the reason I had resisted so long. It certainly was against my own best interest to fight the direction You were leading me. What can I say, Lord? Sometimes I am just not very smart. Thank you for being so patient with me.

Certainly, the benefits of living a life in obedience to You are incredible. You refresh and restore my life, every day. Both my inner self and my physical body are renewed. You fill me with Your Life.

You lead me in paths of righteousness, protecting me from evil snares and leading me away from temptation.

You take away my fears, too, Lord. I have gone through the fire and the floods in obedience to You. In the middle of them, I have discovered that You protect me and that You comfort me - even in the deep, sunless valley of the shadow of death.

You not only protect me from my enemies, Lord, You also honor me in their presence. You dine with me in fellowship before them.

# My Prayer

You anoint me with the oil of Your Spirit.

You overfill my cup with blessings.

Living a life of obedience to You brings me peace, joy, goodness, mercy, and unfailing love all the days of my life. The most wonderful thing of all, Lord is that for the rest of my life I live in sweet fellowship with You—never being alone and never feeling lonely. I am so glad that I am finally learning how to be a sheep!

# Psalm 24

1. The earth is the Lord's and the fullness thereof, the world and those who dwell therein,

2. for he has founded it upon the seas and established it upon the rivers.

3. Who shall ascend the hill of the Lord? And who shall stand in his holy place?

4. He who has clean hands and a pure heart, who does not lift up his soul to what is false and does not swear deceitfully.

5. He will receive blessing from the Lord and righteousness from the God of his salvation.

6. Such is the generation of those who seek him, who seek the face of the God of Jacob.

*Selah*

7. Lift up your heads, O gates! And be lifted up, O ancient doors, that the King of glory may come in.

8. Who is this King of glory? The Lord, strong and mighty, the Lord, mighty in battle!

9. Lift up your heads, O gates! And lift them up, O ancient doors, that the King of glory may come in.

10. Who is this King of glory? The Lord of hosts, he is the King of glory!

*Selah*

# The Earth from Age to Age

Lord, all the earth is Yours. You created it with all of its wonderful wealth of diversity. You established a myriad of marvelous creatures to inhabit it. You founded it upon the heavenly seas and established it in the rivers of time. You gave us dominion over it. Then we messed up everything. What did we do? We opened the door to sin and closed the door of communion with You. What a depressing thought.

Thank You, Lord that You did not leave us in that condition. You sought us out in our rebellion; You gave us a desire to seek You, to renew our communion, to stand before You in Your Holy Place.

No matter how hard we tried, though, we could not recover that fellowship without your help. Our hearts were diseased with the sin nature. Acts of rebellion and evil stained our hands. Only when they are washed in the Blood of the Lamb are we able to have fellowship with You. And those of us who attempt to deceive ourselves by giving lip service to You without a heart change and an obedient life never meet Your conditions to restore the relationship. You give salvation, right standing with You, and the wonderful blessing of fellowship to those of us whose hearts are changed.

Since that very first rebellion, we have been but one long generation of rebels, ignoring what we so foolishly threw away. How stupid it was, Lord, for us to throw away the treasure of Your friendship for the trash of having our own way.

However, this situation will not last. While You gave us dominion over the earth, You retained ownership rights to it. Someday You will be returning to reassert those rights.

I can see the scene in my mind's eye. I can see You, Lord, riding through the ancient gates of Jerusalem. You will not be riding into town as the quiet king on the back of a donkey. No! This time You will come as the King of Glory, The Lord Strong and Mighty, The Lord Mighty in Battle, riding before Your heavenly hosts. Then *everyone* will bow before You. Then everyone will acknowledge Your right to rule. Then You will take Your place as Lord and King of all the earth. What an awesome sight that will be! I can hardly wait. Even so, Lord, come!

# Psalm 25

1 To you, O Lord, I lift up my soul.

2 O my God, in you I trust; let me not be put to shame; let not my enemies exult over me.

3 Indeed, none who wait for you shall be put to shame; they shall be ashamed who are wantonly treacherous.

4 Make me to know your ways, O Lord; teach me your paths.

5 Lead me in your truth and teach me, for you are the God of my salvation; for you I wait all the day long.

6 Remember your mercy, O Lord, and your steadfast love, for they have been from of old.

7 Remember not the sins of my youth or my transgressions; according to your steadfast love remember me, for the sake of your goodness, O Lord!

8 Good and upright is the Lord; therefore he instructs sinners in the way.

9 He leads the humble in what is right, and teaches the humble his way.

10 All the paths of the Lord are steadfast love and faithfulness, for those who keep his covenant and his testimonies.

11 For your name's sake, O Lord, pardon my guilt, for it is great.

12 Who is the man who fears the Lord? Him will he instruct in the way that he should choose.

13 His soul shall abide in well-being, and his offspring shall inherit the land.

# Walking by Faith

Lord, today I want to renew my vow to You:

I freely and willingly give my life to You.

I withhold nothing I am, nothing I have and nothing I do. I gladly die to my life of rebellion so that You might live Your life through me. Oh my God, I place my whole trust in You to enable me to fulfill my vow.

Please work in me to resist the temptation to follow my old friends back into rebellion. I do not want to stand before You in the shame of breaking my vow. Make my fear of shaming You more powerful than the temptation to fall back into my old sinful ways.

I pray for Your support for other people who seriously make this vow, Lord. Work in them to succeed in fulfilling their vows, too. Do not let them be ashamed. Instead, let those who carelessly forsake their vow be ashamed.

Now that I have renewed my vow, Lord, my request is that You show me Your paths. Oh Lord, teach me Your ways. Guide me in Your truth and faithfulness, for You are the God of my salvation. Every day I will wait for Your marching orders - always on call, ready for duty.

I am renewing my vow, Lord because I am an imperfect keeper of it. Please be patient with me and show me Your tender mercy and loving kindness, because I really need them. Please forgive and forget the times when I forget my vow. These are the times when I most need Your mercy and Your steadfast love.

Thank You, Lord, that You willingly teach me Your ways even though I have sometimes failed to follow them. Thank You that when I return to You, You lead me into the right way. Thank You that when I am willing to listen and learn, You eagerly show me Your ways.

14  The friendship of the Lord is for those who fear him, and he makes known to them his covenant.

15  My eyes are ever toward the Lord, for he will pluck my feet out of the net.

16  Turn to me and be gracious to me, for I am lonely and afflicted.

17  The troubles of my heart are enlarged; bring me out of my distresses.

18  Consider my affliction and my trouble, and forgive all my sins.

19  Consider how many are my foes, and with what violent hatred they hate me.

20  Oh, guard my soul, and deliver me! Let me not be put to shame, for I take refuge in you.

21  May integrity and uprightness preserve me, for I wait for you.

22  Redeem Israel, O God, out of all his troubles.

One of the lessons that I am still learning, Lord, is that You pave every path with Your mercy and steadfast love as You guide me in it. It does not matter how dark, dangerous or lonely it may appear. I am learning that I find Your truth and faithfulness on any path where I follow You. I have not completely learned this lesson yet, Lord. So forgive me when my fears keep me from following You down a path I cannot understand. Please remind me then of the wonderful benefits of following You down *any* path:

> You are my teacher,
>
> You give me peace in my heart,
>
> You cause my children to inherit the land, and
>
> You give me Your sweet soul-satisfying companionship as You reveal the deep, inner meaning of Your covenant with me.

So, Lord, when I follow You down one of those scary paths, if I fall into a trap, work in me to trust You to get me out instead of working myself into a panic. If I feel lonely and afflicted, graciously comfort me and give me relief from my feelings of failure. When my heart is troubled, please bring me out of my distress. Behold all of my afflictions and pain and forgive me for feeling sorry for myself and for trying to thrash my own way out of the wilderness. Protect me from my enemies along the path You are leading me, for they will be there with their cruel hatred.

Finally, Lord, when You take me down one of those difficult paths, stay close enough so that I never feel abandoned. When You lead me in, be sure to keep me safe all along the way and deliver me out the other side. I will be going into the path on blind trust and in total faith, so let Your integrity and uprightness preserve and redeem me, Lord, out of all my trouble.

# Psalm 26

1. Vindicate me, O Lord, for I have walked in my integrity, and I have trusted in the Lord without wavering.

2. Prove me, O Lord, and try me; test my heart and my mind.

3. For your steadfast love is before my eyes, and I walk in your faithfulness.

4. I do not sit with men of falsehood, nor do I consort with hypocrites.

5. I hate the assembly of evildoers, and I will not sit with the wicked.

6. I wash my hands in innocence and go around your altar, O Lord,

7. proclaiming thanksgiving aloud, and telling all your wondrous deeds.

8. O Lord, I love the habitation of your house and the place where your glory dwells.

9. Do not sweep my soul away with sinners, nor my life with bloodthirsty men,

10. in whose hands are evil devices, and whose right hands are full of bribes.

11. But as for me, I shall walk in my integrity; redeem me, and be gracious to me.

12. My foot stands on level ground; in the great assembly I will bless the Lord.

# Protection from Harmful Criticism

Lord, when people misunderstand what I am doing, defend me. I am not trying to manipulate anyone; I act with integrity. Every day, I lean on You and focus on You for direction and purpose. I know that will not stop some people from misunderstanding me or from opposing me. So will You please examine me, Lord? Test my heart and my mind to see if I am just fooling myself and if the criticism is accurate. I trust You to tell me if the criticism is justified and I am wrong. I truly want to walk faithfully before You.

I know Lord, that not every critical word helps me. I will be careful to listen only to those whom I trust to have my best interests at heart. I will not socialize with people who show no evidence of loving You, even if they say they are Christians. I will not be close friends with people who go to church just because it is the acceptable thing to do. I will completely avoid people who enjoy doing evil and I will not spend my leisure time with the wicked.

I want to keep all the garbage out of my life, Lord, and spend all my days worshiping You. Then, when You give me an opportunity to tell people how You bless my life, I can rejoice with them in thanksgiving for Your love and mercy. I can gladly share with them what wonderful things You are doing in my life without fearing them.

Lord, I love going to church and worshiping You with all my brothers and sisters in Christ. Please do not ever put me in a place where I cannot go freely to Your house.

Please do not isolate me by putting around me only sinners and bloodthirsty people. It is so much easier to walk in Your way when I know that I am not alone in loving and obeying You. Sharing my life with my spiritual family gives me a firm foundation and provides accountability on the way I am living. Together, we always have abundant reasons for praising You. Thank you for the marvelous gift of Your church.

# Psalm 27

1 The Lord is my light and my salvation; whom shall I fear? The Lord is the stronghold of my life; of whom shall I be afraid?

2 When evildoers assail me to eat up my flesh, my adversaries and foes, it is they who stumble and fall.

3 Though an army encamp against me, my heart shall not fear; though war arise against me, yet I will be confident.

4 One thing have I asked of the Lord, that will I seek after: that I may dwell in the house of the Lord all the days of my life, to gaze upon the beauty of the Lord and to inquire in his temple.

5 For he will hide me in his shelter in the day of trouble; he will conceal me under the cover of his tent; he will lift me high upon a rock.

6 And now my head shall be lifted up above my enemies all around me, and I will offer in his tent sacrifices with shouts of joy; I will sing and make melody to the Lord.

7 Hear, O Lord, when I cry aloud; be gracious to me and answer me!

8 You have said, "Seek my face." My heart says to you, "Your face, Lord, do I seek."

9 Hide not your face from me. Turn not your servant away in anger, O you who have been my help. Cast me not off; forsake me not, O God of my salvation!

10 For my father and my mother have forsaken me, but the Lord will take me in.

11 Teach me your way, O Lord, and lead me on a level path because of my enemies.

# GETTING PAST FEAR

Father, I want to talk to You about my fears. And the first thing I want to say is that I absolutely know - without doubt - that You are my light and my salvation, that You are my refuge and my protection, so I do not *need* to be afraid of anyone or anything. My heart and my mind know that truth. My emotions are another problem altogether. Sometimes fear wants to take over completely.

Situations where I am fearful are the times my enemies try to hurt me through either malicious words or acts of violence. You have been so faithful to protect me in those situations. I am beginning to think that I could face a host of enemies - the way Elisha did - and not feel afraid. My confidence is not in *my* ability to handle the situation. Instead, I have learned by experience that I can trust You to protect me and lean completely on You.

Sometimes I am fearful when trouble unexpectedly pops up: the house floods; my job is at risk; my friend deserts me; the doctor's report is negative. I always experience a flash of fear. Experience has again taught me to turn - very quickly - to You. I immediately talk to You about the problem, turning the whole experience over to You. I trust You to see me through each day. Then I drive out those fearful feelings by singing praise and worship songs to You. That works every time. If I feel the fear coming back over me, I just pray and praise some more. You are always faithful to hear me and to send Your Spirit to comfort me. I have certainly learned that fear cannot stay around when I am in Your presence!

I do have one irrational fear, Lord. Sometimes I am afraid that I will disobey You so much and make You so angry that You will reject me. I know, I know, that really does not make any sense. You love me so much that You gave Your only Son so that I could be part of Your family. Humor me on this one, Lord. As irrational as it is, it drives me closer to Your side. I need You to teach me Your ways and lead me every

12  Give me not up to the will of my adversaries; for false witnesses have risen against me, and they breathe out violence.

13  I believe that I shall look upon the goodness of the Lord in the land of the living!

14  Wait for the Lord; be strong, and let your heart take courage; wait for the Lord!

day so plainly in Your path that there is absolutely no possibility that I might move away from Your presence.

I hate to think what a fear-filled, miserable person I would be if it were not for You, Lord. Your love and ever-watchful care of me makes it possible for me to function in a hostile world. With You as my God, I can be brave and courageous. With You in my heart, it is strong and enduring. With Your Spirit ruling in my life, fear will not control me. Your perfect love casts out my fear.

# Psalm 28

1. To you, O Lord, I call; my rock, be not deaf to me, lest, if you be silent to me, I become like those who go down to the pit.

2. Hear the voice of my pleas for mercy, when I cry to you for help, when I lift up my hands toward your most holy sanctuary.

3. Do not drag me off with the wicked, with the workers of evil, who speak peace with their neighbors while evil is in their hearts.

4. Give to them according to their work and according to the evil of their deeds; give to them according to the work of their hands; render them their due reward.

5. Because they do not regard the works of the Lord or the work of his hands, he will tear them down and build them up no more.

6. Blessed be the Lord! for he has heard the voice of my pleas for mercy.

7. The Lord is my strength and my shield; in him my heart trusts, and I am helped; my heart exults, and with my song I give thanks to him.

8. The Lord is the strength of his people; he is the saving refuge of his anointed.

9. Oh, save your people and bless your heritage! Be their shepherd and carry them forever.

# Smooth-talking Operators

Lord, here I am, crying out to You, again. You know how much I depend on You. If You do not hear me and respond, I am no better off than the living dead. So please listen to me because I *need* You.

Some people, Lord, are really bothering me. I do not want to know them or even be near them. They are smooth-talking operators who are friendly to my face, but they look for every opportunity to stab me in the back. They are wicked people who speak oh-so-sweetly to me in person but who have words of malice and mischief and poison in their hearts.

I know these people will reap what they sow; You will repay them according to what they have done. They will get what they deserve. I do not have to do a thing. You will take care of that because they neither revere You nor obey You. You will break them down, not build them up. I do not want to be near them when it happens. Keep me out of their clutches, Lord.

I know that You have heard my prayer and I thank You for answering it. You are both my Strength for resisting their enticements and my Shield to protect me from becoming their victim. I trust You to do this, so I will put them out of my mind and think of more pleasant things. I will forget about these people and sing songs of praise to You.

> "Lord, You are our unyielding Strength and Our Stronghold of Salvation.
>
> Save Your people and bless Your heritage.
>
> Nourish and shepherd and carry us forever."

# Psalm 29

1. Ascribe to the Lord, O heavenly beings, ascribe to the Lord glory and strength.

2. Ascribe to the Lord the glory due his name; worship the Lord in the splendor of holiness.

3. The voice of the Lord is over the waters; the God of glory thunders, the Lord, over many waters.

4. The voice of the Lord is powerful; the voice of the Lord is full of majesty.

5. The voice of the Lord breaks the cedars; the Lord breaks the cedars of Lebanon.

6. He makes Lebanon to skip like a calf, and Sirion like a young wild ox.

7. The voice of the Lord flashes forth flames of fire.

8. The voice of the Lord shakes the wilderness; the Lord shakes the wilderness of Kadesh.

9. The voice of the Lord makes the deer give birth and strips the forests bare, and in his temple all cry, "Glory!"

10. The Lord sits enthroned over the flood; the Lord sits enthroned as king forever.

11. May the Lord give strength to his people! May the Lord bless his people with peace!

# The Song of the Thunderstorm

Here it comes, Lord! I can see the thunderclouds building up in the west. Look how the sun shines on them. Your glorious splendor covers them. Their mighty power makes me understand just how insignificant and weak we humans really are. Yet, compared to Your own splendor and might, this is nothing. How much more awesome are You, the Creator, than is Your creation!

Listen to the thunder rumbling along beneath the clouds. It is what I imagine that Your voice sounds like—full of power and majesty.

Ah, but Your voice is in the sound of the wind, too. Here it comes, thrashing around in the tops of the trees. Its sibilant whispers sweeping ahead of it anything it finds loose on the ground.

I see the lightning, now, Lord. Suddenly it is there, crackling in the air - then gone, the after-image burning in my eyes. Is that the way You will appear when You return in Your majesty, suddenly flashing across the sky while the whole world trembles and the foundations of the earth shake?

Finally! The curtain of rain is coming this way. The tiny drops rustle like a thousand little feet, followed by big drops bouncing on the hard ground as if quarters dropped on the sidewalk: drops of mercy, showers of blessing.

Oh Lord, what a wonderful smell! That refreshing fragrance, so uniquely its own, of the dry ground soaking up the first drops of moisture. Is that the way the incense of our prayers smell to You? It is such a marvelous and indescribable fragrance.

Now it is raining as if it were the mighty flood of Noah's time. I can hardly see past the front door. One! Two! Three! Four lightning strikes, the thunder so loud and each peal layered one over the other so that even the ears of the dead should be ringing. All of Your creation is saying, "Glory! Glory to God in the highest! You are King over all. You sat as judge at the deluge, You are King of the world, today, You are my King, and You are King of creation forever. Blessed be Your Name!"

# My Prayer

Now it is over. Water drips off the edge of the roof. The sun peeks out. The birds start to sing. Part of a rainbow arcs over the rooftops. Bless Your people, Oh Lord, with peace like the peace that comes after the storm.

# Psalm 30

1. I will extol you, O Lord, for you have drawn me up and have not let my foes rejoice over me.

2. O Lord my God, I cried to you for help, and you have healed me.

3. O Lord, you have brought up my soul from Sheol; you restored me to life from among those who go down to the pit.

4. Sing praises to the Lord, O you his saints, and give thanks to his holy name.

5. For his anger is but for a moment, and his favor is for a lifetime. Weeping may tarry for the night, but joy comes with the morning.

6. As for me, I said in my prosperity, "I shall never be moved."

7. By your favor, O Lord, you made my mountain stand strong; you hid your face; I was dismayed.

8. To you, O Lord, I cry, and to the Lord I plead for mercy:

9. "What profit is there in my death, if I go down to the pit? Will the dust praise you? Will it tell of your faithfulness?

10. Hear, O Lord, and be merciful to me! O Lord, be my helper!"

11. You have turned for me my mourning into dancing; you have loosed my sackcloth and clothed me with gladness,

12. that my glory may sing your praise and not be silent. O Lord my God, I will give thanks to you forever!

# I am Healed!

Lord, I have been telling everyone I know how wonderful You are. I have been talking about You because of what You have done for me. I had been ill for five years. My painful condition was wearing me down and making me discouraged. I praise You, God! You lifted me up. You did not let my enemy win. Instead of the slow death of painful discouragement, You gave me back my life. I cried out to You and You healed me - how awesome is that!

Everyone rejoices with me in singing Your praises. Truly, "in Your favor, there is Life." As David said, "Weeping may endure for a night, but joy comes in the morning." My night was five years long.

I thought that the blessings and prosperity that You had given me would allow me to do anything and everything. Boy was I wrong! I found that out when I got sick. I cried out to You repeatedly, asking You to remove my pain and suffering. I reminded You of the work You had given me to do. I could not complete it as sick as I was. I asked repeatedly for You to show me mercy and to help me. You heard me. You turned my sorrow into rejoicing. You have swept away my pain and filled me with gladness.

To the end of time, my tongue and my heart and everything glorious within me will sing Your praises and not be silent. Oh Lord, my God, I will give You thanks forever!

# Psalm 31

1 In you, O Lord, do I take refuge; let me never be put to shame; in your righteousness deliver me!

2 Incline your ear to me; rescue me speedily! Be a rock of refuge for me, a strong fortress to save me!

3 For you are my rock and my fortress; and for your name's sake you lead me and guide me;

4 you take me out of the net they have hidden for me, for you are my refuge.

5 Into your hand I commit my spirit; you have redeemed me, O Lord, faithful God.

6 I hate those who pay regard to worthless idols, but I trust in the Lord.

7 I will rejoice and be glad in your steadfast love, because you have seen my affliction; you have known the distress of my soul,

8 and you have not delivered me into the hand of the enemy; you have set my feet in a broad place.

9 Be gracious to me, O Lord, for I am in distress; my eye is wasted from grief; my soul and my body also.

10 For my life is spent with sorrow, and my years with sighing; my strength fails because of my iniquity, and my bones waste away.

11 Because of all my adversaries I have become a reproach, especially to my neighbors, and an object of dread to my acquaintances; those who see me in the street flee from me.

12 I have been forgotten like one who is dead; I have become like a broken vessel.

# Forgiveness for Sin

Here I am, looking for You, again, Lord. I need Your help. I need Your deliverance! Please do not disappoint me. Hear my prayer and deliver me quickly, because I need You to come to my rescue. I trust You - because You are my Rock and my Refuge - to lead me out of the mess I'm in and to get me back on the path where You want me to be.

You know what the problem is, Lord. I fell into a sin-trap that my enemies set up for me. I let temptation lure me into doing what I know was wrong.

As guilty and as condemned as I feel, I know that I am not beyond forgiveness. After all, I long ago committed my spirit into Your hands. By the blood sacrifice of Your Son, You redeemed me, Oh Lord. Even though I have done wrong and sinned against You, I am not going to turn away from You, because I trust You.

The problem is that my sin has robbed me of Your sweet fellowship. You see how this has afflicted and distressed me. I know that You haven't stopped loving me or showing me Your grace because I've failed You. You continue to keep me safe, and I still have all the blessings You gave me - except for this one.

Oh, how I need Your mercy, Lord! My sin has brought about this distance between us. It has given me grief that has weakened my eyes, my soul and my body. Now I spend my life in sorrow and my years with sighing. The grief and trouble of my sin has robbed me of my strength. Even my bones are wasting away.

This sin has made me such a miserable person that my enemies are pointing me out as a bad example. My neighbors and acquaintances dread to see me. They make excuses and run away from me on the street! I feel numb on the inside and forgotten by the world. Now, fear has come in and I feel afraid for my life!

13 For I hear the whispering of many—terror on every side!—as they scheme together against me, as they plot to take my life.

14 But I trust in you, O Lord; I say, "You are my God."

15 My times are in your hand; rescue me from the hand of my enemies and from my persecutors!

16 Make your face shine on your servant; save me in your steadfast love!

17 O Lord, let me not be put to shame, for I call upon you; let the wicked be put to shame; let them go silently to Sheol.

18 Let the lying lips be mute, which speak insolently against the righteous in pride and contempt.

19 Oh, how abundant is your goodness, which you have stored up for those who fear you and worked for those who take refuge in you, in the sight of the children of mankind!

20 In the cover of your presence you hide them from the plots of men; you store them in your shelter from the strife of tongues.

21 Blessed be the Lord, for he has wondrously shown his steadfast love to me when I was in a besieged city.

22 I had said in my alarm, "I am cut off from your sight." But you heard the voice of my pleas for mercy when I cried to you for help.

23 Love the Lord, all you his saints! The Lord preserves the faithful but abundantly repays the one who acts in pride.

24 Be strong, and let your heart take courage, all you who wait for the Lord!

This is where You come in. Right now, I repent of my sin and turn back to You. You are my God. I committed my whole life to You and now I am renewing that commitment. I am asking You to forgive me. Release me from these feelings of guilt and condemnation. Deliver me from the trouble that has come out of my sin. Silence my enemies' lies. They speak the truth about me when they talk about my sin. But when they say that it is too late for You to forgive me and for You to redeem the situation I know they are lying.

You have goodness piled up in Your storehouse for those who reverently fear You and who worship You in spirit and in truth. You honor those who repent and turn away from their sin with the sweet joy of Your fellowship. This marvelous goodness of Your presence You have designed just for those who claim Your cleansing from their sin. Your companionship is not the only thing that You reserve for those who confess You as their God. You hide them in Your secret place. You put them in Your private pavilion to keep them safe. I am one of those people!

Blessed is Your Name, Oh Lord! For You have shown me Your marvelous loving favor when I was cut off by my sin. You have forgiven me. You restored to me Your sweet fellowship.

I will tell everyone to love You. I will tell them how You mercifully preserve those who worship You in faith and in truth. I will tell them to be strong and to resist temptation. I will tell them that if they fall into a sin-trap that You will rescue them.

Blessed be the Name of the Lord!

# Psalm 32

1. Blessed is the one whose transgression is forgiven, whose sin is covered.

2. Blessed is the man against whom the Lord counts no iniquity, and in whose spirit there is no deceit.

3. For when I kept silent, my bones wasted away through my groaning all day long.

4. For day and night your hand was heavy upon me; my strength was dried up as by the heat of summer. *Selah*

5. I acknowledged my sin to you, and I did not cover my iniquity; I said, "I will confess my transgressions to the Lord," and you forgave the iniquity of my sin.

*Selah*

6. Therefore let everyone who is godly offer prayer to you at a time when you may be found; surely in the rush of great waters, they shall not reach him.

7. You are a hiding place for me; you preserve me from trouble; you surround me with shouts of deliverance.

*Selah*

8. I will instruct you and teach you in the way you should go; I will counsel you with my eye upon you.

9. Be not like a horse or a mule, without understanding, which must be curbed with bit and bridle, or it will not stay near you.

10. Many are the sorrows of the wicked, but steadfast love surrounds the one who trusts in the Lord.

11. Be glad in the Lord, and rejoice, O righteous, and shout for joy, all you upright in heart!

# Reflecting on Forgiveness

Lord, what a wonderful gift You have given me - forgiveness. Yet I cannot live so perfectly that I always obey You. Nevertheless, You made a way for me to recover from the times that I do fail. When I admit to You that I have sinned, You forgive me and erase my iniquity. You restore our fellowship.

Sometimes it takes a while for me to get over my stubborn pride or foolish rebellion and come to You about my sin. Until I confess my sin to You, I really suffer for it. I am in a terrible mood, my guilt saturates me and I feel as if my bones are wasting away. Day and night, I feel how I have grieved Your Spirit. My sin stops the flow of our relationship as if water shut off at a faucet. My soul feels like it is scorching in the dessert. It happens every time, but somehow I always forget how terrible it is.

What I do not forget, though, is what happens when I acknowledge my sin. When I finally make up my mind to stop trying to hide what I have done and admit everything, You do the most amazing thing. You *instantly* restore our fellowship! No rebukes. No cold shoulders. No leaving me to wonder if once again You will forgive me. Just instant restoration of our fellowship. Just a loving welcome home. Wow! That really blows me away.

Lord, I know that I should always obey You. When I fail, I should not be slow to seek Your forgiveness. If for no other reason, I need to stay "prayed up" so that when the floods of trials come in, they will not overwhelm my spirit. I know from experience that the only place to be when trials come is in the hiding place You provide for me. There You preserve me, surrounding me with songs of deliverance and shouts of joy.

I hear what You are saying; You will instruct me and teach me in the way I should go. You will keep Your eye on me. You want to do all of this for me if I just will not let my stubborn pride and rebellion get in the way, if I will not let my sin get between us. Instead of running *away* from You when I sin, You want me to trust You enough to run *toward* You.

# My Prayer

Lord, I do not want to sin, but if I do, please help me to remember which way to run! Help me to stay close to You so that You can surround me with Your mercy and loving-kindness. Let me live every day in Your forgiveness, rejoicing in Your friendship, and shouting for joy at being at peace with You, my God.

# Psalm 33

1 Shout for joy in the Lord, O you righteous! Praise befits the upright.

2 Give thanks to the Lord with the lyre; make melody to him with the harp of ten strings!

3 Sing to him a new song; play skillfully on the strings, with loud shouts.

4 For the word of the Lord is upright, and all his work is done in faithfulness.

5 He loves righteousness and justice; the earth is full of the steadfast love of the Lord.

6 By the word of the Lord the heavens were made, and by the breath of his mouth all their host.

7 He gathers the waters of the sea as a heap; he puts the deeps in storehouses.

8 Let all the earth fear the Lord; let all the inhabitants of the world stand in awe of him!

9 For he spoke, and it came to be; he commanded, and it stood firm.

10 The Lord brings the counsel of the nations to nothing; he frustrates the plans of the peoples.

11 The counsel of the Lord stands forever, the plans of his heart to all generations.

12 Blessed is the nation whose God is the Lord, the people whom he has chosen as his heritage!

13 The Lord looks down from heaven; he sees all the children of man;

# The Power of God's Spoken Word

I rejoice in Your presence, today, Lord. I praise You for Who You Are - my God, my Sovereign, my Redeemer, my Creator. I thank You for all that You do in my life. I sing Your praises in my spirit and with my mouth. You have blessed me, blessed me, and blessed me, again. You speak Your Word to me and it saturates me in Your loving-kindness.

Your Word is so powerful, Lord. By Your Word You made the heavens and all the millions of stars, the planets and all that surrounds them. By Your Word, You put boundaries upon the seas, making them the proper depth.

If only we truly understood the magnificent power of Your Word. Our understanding would cause everyone on earth to praise and worship You. Everyone would honor You, for when You speak, things happen. When You command, the work stands fast. When You speak, all the weighty discussions of the nations make no difference. The thoughts and plans of the people count as nothing.

What *really* matters is what You tell us. Your council stands forever. The thoughts of Your heart hold fast over generations. Our nation rises or falls by Your Word. You bless our country when we remember that we are one nation under God and when we fear You because of it. All our citizens do not know this truth, but if Your children would live as if they trusted in the power of Your Word, how different our lives would be.

You search the world, looking for a people who will live their lives based on the power of Your Word. Does our country live that way? No, instead, we depend on our army, our technology, anything except You. None of the things we trust to protect us and give us security can give us victory. No one else has the power to deliver us.

You want to deliver us, Lord. You look for people who honor You and worship You with awe. When You find those who wait for You to speak Your Word, when you find those who have their hope in Your mercy

14 from where he sits enthroned he looks out on all the inhabitants of the earth,

15 he who fashions the hearts of them all and observes all their deeds.

16 The king is not saved by his great army; a warrior is not delivered by his great strength.

17 The war horse is a false hope for salvation, and by its great might it cannot rescue.

18 Behold, the eye of the Lord is on those who fear him, on those who hope in his steadfast love,

19 that he may deliver their soul from death and keep them alive in famine.

20 Our soul waits for the Lord; he is our help and our shield.

21 For our heart is glad in him, because we trust in his holy name.

22 Let your steadfast love, O Lord, be upon us, even as we hope in you.

and loving-kindness, You deliver them. You deliver them from being apart from You and from the slavery of fear.

So, today, Lord, I wait expectantly for Your Word. I look to You for my protection because I trust in You. My heart rejoices in Your Holy Name.

Let Your mercy and Your loving-kindness, Oh Lord, be upon me in proportion to Your love. Bless me, Lord with Your Word. Bless me, indeed.

# Psalm 34

1 I will bless the Lord at all times; his praise shall continually be in my mouth.

2 My soul makes its boast in the Lord; let the humble hear and be glad.

3 Oh, magnify the Lord with me, and let us exalt his name together!

4 I sought the Lord, and he answered me and delivered me from all my fears.

5 Those who look to him are radiant, and their faces shall never be ashamed.

6 This poor man cried, and the Lord heard him and saved him out of all his troubles.

7 The angel of the Lord encamps around those who fear him, and delivers them.

8 Oh, taste and see that the Lord is good! Blessed is the man who takes refuge in him!

9 Oh, fear the Lord, you his saints, for those who fear him have no lack!

10 The young lions suffer want and hunger; but those who seek the Lord lack no good thing.

11 Come, O children, listen to me; I will teach you the fear of the Lord.

12 What man is there who desires life and loves many days, that he may see good?

13 Keep your tongue from evil and your lips from speaking deceit.

# Freedom from Overwhelming Fear

Lord, I will bless You all the time. I will praise Your Name continually. I will boast of the wonderful ways You work in my life. The humble will be glad for me and will seek You for themselves. When they, too, see You at work in their lives, then we will magnify You and we will exalt Your name together.

What filled me with joy? I sought You, praying fervently. You heard me and delivered me from all my fears. That is why I have this big smile on my face and this joy in my heart. I am not afraid, anymore! I cried out and You saved me from all my troubles.

Indeed, You not only delivered me from all my fears, You replaced them with a "fear" of You. When I stopped zooming in my focus on all the things that made me afraid, when I turned my eyes toward You and worshiped You with the reverence and awe You deserve, then I had no place for my fears. Why? Because the presence of Your Holy Spirit drove them out! Praise Your Holy Name! I have tasted the fear of the Lord and found it good. I had much rather have this breath-taking fear of You in my life than to be afraid of anything else. Feeling this awe and reverence for You is so much better than feeling the lonely, empty, panicky feeling of all my other fears.

I have learned this lesson well, Lord. I will not look for things to fear. Instead, when I need something I will ask You for it, and then I will trust You to supply it. Instead of spending my time thinking about the scary parts of life, I will worship You. I will teach my children this, too, so that they will learn to fear You instead of fearing everything else.

Father, this will make a significant change in my life. I have spent a lot of time thinking and talking about all the things that I fear. I do not want to do that any more. I see how unhealthy it is to live that way. I have tasted the peace that comes from looking to You. Lord, give me

14 Turn away from evil and do good; seek peace and pursue it.

15 The eyes of the Lord are toward the righteous and his ears toward their cry.

16 The face of the Lord is against those who do evil, to cut off the memory of them from the earth.

17 When the righteous cry for help, the Lord hears and delivers them out of all their troubles.

18 The Lord is near to the brokenhearted and saves the crushed in spirit.

19 Many are the afflictions of the righteous, but the Lord delivers him out of them all.

20 He keeps all his bones; not one of them is broken.

21 Affliction will slay the wicked, and those who hate the righteous will be condemned.

22 The Lord redeems the life of his servants; none of those who take refuge in him will be condemned.

such a craving for that peace to be an everyday part of my life that I will not fall into the old habits of fear.

Lord, You love the people who put their trust in You. However, You cut Yourself off from those who try to do everything for themselves, ignoring You and the abundant blessings that You want to provide for them. I do not want to be cut off from You that way. When I am feeling distressed or troubled, I will cry out to You for help. I will not wait and try to fix it myself. I know that the sooner I ask for Your help, the sooner I will get it. Turning quickly to You will give my fears no time to take over.

I know that my overwhelming fears do not honor You, Lord. Jesus died so that I might not be a slave to the fear of death. I know that unhealthy fears are just another way I express my rebellion and disobedience when fear keeps me from being at peace with You. I am sorry, Lord, that I ever let fear control me. I regret all the times when I let my fear get bigger than my faith in You.

Father, the next time I feel afraid, do not let it separate me from You. Instead, use it to remind me that You will deliver me out of all the evil that confronts me. Put in me the absolute certainty that while evil will cause the death of the wicked, You will not let evil so much as break one of my bones, for You are my Redeemer, my Refuge, and my Peace.

# Psalm 35

1. Contend, O Lord, with those who contend with me; fight against those who fight against me!
2. Take hold of shield and buckler and rise for my help!
3. Draw the spear and javelin against my pursuers! Say to my soul, "I am your salvation!"
4. Let them be put to shame and dishonor who seek after my life! Let them be turned back and disappointed who devise evil against me!
5. Let them be like chaff before the wind, with the angel of the Lord driving them away!
6. Let their way be dark and slippery, with the angel of the Lord pursuing them!
7. For without cause they hid their net for me; without cause they dug a pit for my life.
8. Let destruction come upon him when he does not know it! And let the net that he hid ensnare him; let him fall into it—to his destruction!
9. Then my soul will rejoice in the Lord, exulting in his salvation.
10. All my bones shall say, "O Lord, who is like you, delivering the poor from him who is too strong for him, the poor and needy from him who robs him?"
11. Malicious witnesses rise up; they ask me of things that I do not know.
12. They repay me evil for good; my soul is bereft.
13. But I, when they were sick—I wore sackcloth; I afflicted myself with fasting; I prayed with head bowed on my chest.

# Death by Gossip

Contend, Oh Lord, with those who contend with me. I am in a spiritual battle like none I have ever fought. Fight against those who fight against me. Stand up for me! Send Your angels to deliver me! Dishonor those who seek my life and confound those who plan my hurt. Blow them away to some dark and slippery place. They set a trap for me for absolutely no reason—so let them fall into their own trap!

The day I see them fall will be the day I rejoice that my deliverance has come from You. Everything within me will rejoice and I will say, "Lord, who is like You? Who is too strong for You? Who will seize the poor and afflicted away from You? Yes, who is like You? You deliver the poor and the needy from enemies who snatch away his good name."

Lord, You know what is happening. Malicious witnesses rise up and try to snarl me in the web of their words. These people are repaying the good that I did for them with this evil attack. When they were down and out, I stood by them and did what I could to relieve their suffering. Look what has happened, now. The evil one is using them to destroy me. I am having trouble and instead of coming to my defense, they have come to ruin my reputation! They gather to slander my name and to gossip about me, rejoicing in my troubles. They make sick jokes and sly remarks to me. Lord, I do not even recognize the people that I thought were my friends.

Lord, how long are You going to let them get away with this? (Rescue me and I will publicly praise Your Name in Your House.) Do not let these false friends entertain each other with my problems. Do not let them invent stories that blow everything out of proportion. I can just hear them now, "Just wait until I tell you what I saw!"

You have seen this Lord, You know it is true!

Wake up, Lord, and reach out on my behalf. Give me justice and vindicate me, O Lord my God, according to Your righteousness. Do not let these hypocrites have the satisfaction of seeing their gossip destroy

14 I went about as though I grieved for my friend or my brother; as one who laments his mother, I bowed down in mourning.

15 But at my stumbling they rejoiced and gathered; they gathered together against me; wretches whom I did not know tore at me without ceasing;

16 like profane mockers at a feast, they gnash at me with their teeth.

17 How long, O Lord, will you look on? Rescue me from their destruction, my precious life from the lions!

18 I will thank you in the great congregation; in the mighty throng I will praise you.

19 Let not those rejoice over me who are wrongfully my foes, and let not those wink the eye who hate me without cause.

20 For they do not speak peace, but against those who are quiet in the land they devise words of deceit.

21 They open wide their mouths against me; they say, "Aha, Aha! our eyes have seen it!"

22 You have seen, O Lord; be not silent! O Lord, be not far from me!

23 Awake and rouse yourself for my vindication, for my cause, my God and my Lord!

24 Vindicate me, O Lord, my God, according to your righteousness, and let them not rejoice over me!

25 Let them not say in their hearts, "Aha, our heart's desire!" Let them not say, "We have swallowed him up."

26 Let them be put to shame and disappointed altogether who rejoice at my calamity! Let them be clothed with shame and dishonor who magnify themselves against me!

27 Let those who delight in my righteousness shout for joy and be glad and say evermore, "Great is the Lord, who delights in the welfare of his servant!"

28 Then my tongue shall tell of your righteousness and of your praise all the day long.

my reputation. Do not let me die by gossip! Instead, drive the evil one away from them so that the shame and dishonor they are heaping on my back does not fall upon their own heads.

I do have some true friends, Lord. They have probably heard the stories, but they neither believe them nor spread them. They know the truth and believe in my integrity. Let them laugh at how ridiculous the stories are. Let them tell everyone that I am Your true servant and that You still take pleasure in me.

As for me - I have no time to gossip. My tongue is too busy talking about Your righteousness and justice. I tell every one that I have reasons to praise You every minute of the day. That is a lot more satisfying than spreading gossip.

# Psalm 36

1 Transgression speaks to the wicked deep in his heart; there is no fear of God before his eyes.

2 For he flatters himself in his own eyes that his iniquity cannot be found out and hated.

3 The words of his mouth are trouble and deceit; he has ceased to act wisely and do good.

4 He plots trouble while on his bed; he sets himself in a way that is not good; he does not reject evil.

5 Your steadfast love, O Lord, extends to the heavens, your faithfulness to the clouds.

6 Your righteousness is like the mountains of God; your judgments are like the great deep; man and beast you save, O Lord.

7 How precious is your steadfast love, O God! The children of mankind take refuge in the shadow of your wings.

8 They feast on the abundance of your house, and you give them drink from the river of your delights.

9 For with you is the fountain of life; in your light do we see light.

10 Oh, continue your steadfast love to those who know you, and your righteousness to the upright of heart!

11 Let not the foot of arrogance come upon me, nor the hand of the wicked drive me away.

12 There the evildoers lie fallen; they are thrust down, unable to rise.

# The Desire to Destroy

What is it Lord, that draws some people to evil? The desire to destroy is like a siren's song, calling deeply to their hearts. It is so compelling that they do not even consider You. They convince themselves that they can do all kinds of evil things and face no consequences. They talk about their evil plans, even plotting ways to do evil while still in their beds. Sin twists their minds so they do not reject evil. Instead, they purposely seek it out.

Why is it Lord, that some people reject You in favor of evil? Your mercy and loving-kindness continue to extend to them even while they are committing their evil acts. Your righteousness is like a mountain before them. Why do they ignore it? Your voice is calling them even as they hatch their evil desires. Even when they are rushing to destroy, You call out to them. No crime is too great, no perversity too vile for You to seek them.

Why do some people make evil their god instead of believing in You? Instead of hate, they would have Your precious love. No longer imprisoned by greed and lust, You would give them freedom. They would no longer be starving on crumbs of self-indulgence; they would be feasting on the abundance of Your house. In place of poisoned water to drink, You would quench their thirst from Your river of delights. While they seek death, You offer them the fountain of life. They hide in darkness when You send Your Light.

Why Lord, do You not give up on them? You continue to offer the gift of salvation for everyone whose ways are evil. Why do they continually refuse this precious gift? Why do they reject Your love, resent Your power and rejoice in doing evil?

Is Your heart breaking Lord, because those who choose to live in darkness refuse Your love? Will the day soon come when You no longer strive with those who choose evil? The way they live hardens their hearts. They strike out against people who love You and drive away everyone who shows them Your love. They become deafened to Your call.

Oh, that they might hear and see before the Day of Judgment comes when those who do evil lay fallen, thrown down, never to rise. Oh, what a day of horror for those who reject You!

# Psalm 37

1 Fret not yourself because of evildoers; be not envious of wrongdoers!

2 For they will soon fade like the grass and wither like the green herb.

3 Trust in the Lord, and do good; dwell in the land and befriend faithfulness.

4 Delight yourself in the Lord, and he will give you the desires of your heart.

5 Commit your way to the Lord; trust in him, and he will act.

6 He will bring forth your righteousness as the light, and your justice as the noonday.

7 Be still before the Lord and wait patiently for him; fret not yourself over the one who prospers in his way, over the man who carries out evil devices!

8 Refrain from anger, and forsake wrath! Fret not yourself; it tends only to evil.

9 For the evildoers shall be cut off, but those who wait for the Lord shall inherit the land.

10 In just a little while, the wicked will be no more; though you look carefully at his place, he will not be there.

11 But the meek shall inherit the land and delight themselves in abundant peace.

12 The wicked plots against the righteous and gnashes his teeth at him,

13 but the Lord laughs at the wicked, for he sees that his day is coming.

# Futile Fretting

Lord, I must admit there are times—like now—when the injustice of the world really gets to me. I fret because You do not immediately punish evil men. I envy the rich and famous that seem to get away with everything. Life is just not fair! You tell me not to fret or envy them and that You will soon cast them down. Well, when is "soon?" I would like to see that happen while the report of their evil activity is still fresh in everyone's minds.

I know. I know. All this fretting and envy is not Your way for me. Instead of fretting, You want me to trust You to handle the situation. You even give me good reasons to live this way. You promise to establish me in the land and feed me on Your faithfulness. That is good motivation for obeying You!

If that were not enough, You said that if I delight myself in You instead of spending my time fretting over injustice, You would give me the desires of my heart. Wow! I like spending time with You, and I do not enjoy feeling fretful and unhappy, so maybe changing my attitude will not be so hard, after all.

Besides, You also say that if I give up these negative feelings and commit my ways to You I can trust You to resolve the injustice. To top that off, You will make my own life a shining example of uprightness and justice. That really appeals to me, Lord, because it is the only way I see to make any impact on the world's injustice.

I know from experience that I can trust You. In my mind, I know the best plan is to be still and rest in You. If I patiently lean upon You, I will see You act. Certainly this fretting over people who are prospering as they carry out their wicked plans does me no good.

At best, fretting makes me feel miserable. At worst, the feeling could cause me to attempt some foolhardy action that would not help anyone.

14 The wicked draw the sword and bend their bows to bring down the poor and needy, to slay those whose way is upright;

15 their sword shall enter their own heart, and their bows shall be broken.

16 Better is the little that the righteous has than the abundance of many wicked.

17 For the arms of the wicked shall be broken, but the Lord upholds the righteous.

18 The Lord knows the days of the blameless, and their heritage will remain forever;

19 they are not put to shame in evil times; in the days of famine they have abundance.

20 But the wicked will perish; the enemies of the Lord are like the glory of the pastures; they vanish—like smoke they vanish away.

21 The wicked borrows but does not pay back, but the righteous is generous and gives;

22 for those blessed by the Lord shall inherit the land, but those cursed by him shall be cut off.

23 The steps of a man are established by the Lord, when he delights in his way;

24 though he fall, he shall not be cast headlong, for the Lord upholds his hand.

25 I have been young, and now am old, yet I have not seen the righteous forsaken or his children begging for bread.

26 He is ever lending generously, and his children become a blessing.

27 Turn away from evil and do good; so shall you dwell forever.

28 For the Lord loves justice; he will not forsake his saints. They are preserved forever, but the children of the wicked shall be cut off.

Instead, I will think about the long-term consequences of evil that You have shown me in the Bible. I will remember that those who put their trust in You will inherit the earth.

You will cut off those who do evil. They will be gone from the place where they flourished. When I see the wicked plotting against the righteous, I will remember that You are laughing at their plans. You see their day of defeat coming. When I hear that the wicked are setting out to destroy the poor and the needy, I will remember that their weapons will enter their own hearts and You will destroy them.

If You want me to do something about this situation, just say the word. I will be happy to be Your hands and feet if You will tell me what You want me to do.

In the meantime, replace my envy for the abundance of those who are wicked with contentment with Your provision. When judgment comes, their abundance will not save them, any more than it would save me. Instead, You will uphold the person who depends on You. I want to be that person. I want to be upright and blameless before You. I want You to be in charge of all my days. That way I know that I will have an eternal inheritance. I know in times of evil, You will not shame me and in times of famine You will satisfy me.

The time of evil is now, and we certainly have a famine of righteousness. Even so, I am satisfied that You are in total control. I know that the wicked will perish. They will vanish like smoke up the chimney. Their abundance will turn into need. They will have to borrow and they will not be able to repay.

On the other hand, those who trust in You will not only have enough to meet their own needs, but will also have enough to lend others. Their lending to others pleases You so much that You bless their children!

That is the kind of life I want, Lord. I want You to direct my steps, so that when I fall - as I know that I will - You will be there to help me up. I know that You do not forsake those who are righteous, for You delight in justice.

29 The righteous shall inherit the land and dwell upon it forever.

30 The mouth of the righteous utters wisdom, and his tongue speaks justice.

31 The law of his God is in his heart; his steps do not slip.

32 The wicked watches for the righteous and seeks to put him to death.

33 The Lord will not abandon him to his power or let him be condemned when he is brought to trial.

34 Wait for the Lord and keep his way, and he will exalt you to inherit the land; you will look on when the wicked are cut off.

35 I have seen a wicked, ruthless man, spreading himself like a green laurel tree.

36 But he passed away, and behold, he was no more; though I sought him, he could not be found.

37 Mark the blameless and behold the upright, for there is a future for the man of peace.

38 But transgressors shall be altogether destroyed; the future of the wicked shall be cut off.

39 The salvation of the righteous is from the Lord; he is their stronghold in the time of trouble.

40 The Lord helps them and delivers them; he delivers them from the wicked and saves them, because they take refuge in him.

Therefore, no matter how injustice seems to flourish, I will keep my mouth full of Your praises, my heart filled with Your Word, and my steps on the path You have given me. I trust You to preserve me, and in Your perfect time, to cut off the wicked and to destroy them altogether. Your Word is true and You faithfully keep all Your promises.

# Psalm 38

1 O Lord, rebuke me not in your anger, nor discipline me in your wrath!

2 For your arrows have sunk into me, and your hand has come down on me.

3 There is no soundness in my flesh because of your indignation; there is no health in my bones because of my sin.

4 For my iniquities have gone over my head; like a heavy burden, they are too heavy for me.

5 My wounds stink and fester because of my foolishness,

6 I am utterly bowed down and prostrate; all the day I go about mourning.

7 For my sides are filled with burning, and there is no soundness in my flesh.

8 I am feeble and crushed; I groan because of the tumult of my heart.

9 O Lord, all my longing is before you; my sighing is not hidden from you.

10 My heart throbs; my strength fails me, and the light of my eyes—it also has gone from me.

11 My friends and companions stand aloof from my plague, and my nearest kin stand far off.

12 Those who seek my life lay their snares; those who seek my hurt speak of ruin and meditate treachery all day long.

13 But I am like a deaf man; I do not hear, like a mute man who does not open his mouth.

# Cry of Repentance

Lord, You have every right to be angry and to punish me severely, because I have really blown it, this time. Before the words were out of my mouth, before I had completed my sin, Your Holy Spirit convicted me that I had willfully sinned - *again*!

Lord, what am I going to do? I know this is wrong, and I do not want to do it. It is tearing me up inside to so easily fall into this sin. I feel like I am drowning, sinking to the very bottom of the ocean with thousand pound shoes on my feet. When I look into the mirror, the foolish person looking back at me revolts me. This is so depressing. My sin is making me physically ill. I feel cold all the time and exhausted.

Lord, You see all of this. You know my guilt and the grief I feel for sinning. My heart bleeds; I have no strength left, and the joy has gone out of my life. I feel so very miserable that people who love me stay away and my friends and neighbors avoid me.

Worse than that, my sin has given an opportunity to my enemies to plot against me. They search for ways to drive me even further away from You.

I know what I am doing to myself, but I cannot seem to help it. My sin has made me so miserable that I am not able to speak peacefully to my friends. I cannot resist the plotting of my enemies or speak out in my own defense. At this point, all I can do is throw myself on Your mercy and trust You to protect me in spite of the mess in which I have gotten myself. I am asking You to keep my enemies from taking advantage of my situation.

I have had enough of this misery, even though it is not one-tenth of what I deserve. Lord, I confess that I am guilty and full of iniquity. I am sorry that I sinned. I repent of my sin against You and I ask that You give me the ability never to repeat it. Look at all the temptations and vigorous enemies that I have against me and take pity on me.

Cleanse me, Father, and renew Your fellowship with me. Make haste to help me, Lord, for You are my salvation.

14 I have become like a man who does not hear, and in whose mouth are no rebukes.

15 But for you, O Lord, do I wait; it is you, O Lord my God, who will answer.

16 For I said, "Only let them not rejoice over me, who boast against me when my foot slips!"

17 For I am ready to fall, and my pain is ever before me.

18 I confess my iniquity; I am sorry for my sin.

19 But my foes are vigorous, they are mighty, and many are those who hate me wrongfully.

20 Those who render me evil for good accuse me because I follow after good.

21 Do not forsake me, O Lord! O my God, be not far from me!

22 Make haste to help me, O Lord, my salvation!

# My Prayer

# Psalm 39

1  I said, "I will guard my ways, that I may not sin with my tongue; I will guard my mouth with a muzzle, so long as the wicked are in my presence."

2  I was mute and silent; I held my peace to no avail, and my distress grew worse.

3  My heart became hot within me. As I mused, the fire burned; then I spoke with my tongue:

4  "O Lord, make me know my end and what is the measure of my days; let me know how fleeting I am!

5  Behold, you have made my days a few handbreadths, and my lifetime is as nothing before you. Surely all mankind stands as a mere breath!

*Selah*

6  Surely a man goes about as a shadow! Surely for nothing they are in turmoil; man heaps up wealth and does not know who will gather!

7  "And now, O Lord, for what do I wait? My hope is in you.

8  Deliver me from all my transgressions. Do not make me the scorn of the fool!

9  I am mute; I do not open my mouth, for it is you who have done it.

10  Remove your stroke from me; I am spent by the hostility of your hand.

11  When you discipline a man with rebukes for sin, you consume like a moth what is dear to him; **O** surely all mankind is a mere breath!

*Selah*

# Open Mouth, Insert Foot

Lord, why do I let my mouth get me in so much trouble? I knew that I was going into an explosive situation. I even decided in advance to watch very carefully every word I spoke and to keep a tight rein on my tongue. I tried, Lord, I really did. Yet, as I sat there listening to these foolish - even evil - people, I got so angry and disgusted that I just erupted. Just as an erupting volcano spews fire and brimstone over everything, all I did was worsen the situation as I spoke. Now I am disgusted with myself.

Lord, You know me. You know my weaknesses and shortcomings. Even at my best, I am merely a short breath in Your sight. Some days, I feel like a shadow in a pantomime, my life meaningless and futile because I mess up so often.

If my life has any meaning, Lord, it comes from You. So please, when I blow up, the way I did, today, forgive me quickly. My life is too short to spend it feeling forever guilty. Hear my confession quickly, Lord, and restore my joy. Give me strength and encouragement to speak more gently next time, and give me Your fellowship to enjoy while I am still on this earth.

**12** "Hear my prayer, O Lord, and give ear to my cry; hold not your peace at my tears! For I am a sojourner with you, a guest, like all my fathers.

**13** Look away from me, that I may smile again, before I depart and am no more!"

# My Prayer

*Changing Me, Change the World*

# Psalm 40

1. I waited patiently for the Lord; he inclined to me and heard my cry.

2. He drew me up from the pit of destruction, out of the miry bog, and set my feet upon a rock, making my steps secure.

3. He put a new song in my mouth, a song of praise to our God. Many will see and fear, and put their trust in the Lord.

4. Blessed is the man who makes the Lord his trust, who does not turn to the proud, to those who go astray after a lie!

5. You have multiplied, O Lord my God, your wondrous deeds and your thoughts toward us; none can compare with you! I will proclaim and tell of them, yet they are more than can be told.

6. Sacrifice and offering you have not desired, but you have given me an open ear. Burnt offering and sin offering you have not required.

7. Then I said, "Behold, I have come; in the scroll of the book it is written of me:

8. I desire to do your will, O my God; your law is within my heart."

9. I have told the glad news of deliverance in the great congregation; behold, I have not restrained my lips, as you know, O Lord.

10. I have not hidden your deliverance within my heart; I have spoken of your faithfulness and your salvation; I have not concealed your steadfast love and your faithfulness from the great congregation.

11. As for you, O Lord, you will not restrain your mercy from me; your steadfast love and your faithfulness will ever preserve me!

# GRATITUDE FOR DELIVERANCE

Whew! Lord, I thought that I was never going to get through that. I tried very hard to be patient and to wait for You to work things out Your way. Even so, You must have gotten tired of hearing me cry for deliverance. Finally, You drew me out of a horrible pit of tumult and destruction. Drawing me out of that sticky clay, You set my feet upon the Rock, steadying my steps and establishing my ways.

That was a double blessing. You put a new praise song in my mouth at the same time. I shall sing of Your deliverance so that many will fear You and put their trust in You. For my endurance, You gave me the prize reserved for those who trust in You instead of trusting false gods or on their own work for deliverance. Thank you, Lord.

When I reflect on Your grace and goodness to me, I remember that this is just another in a long list of blessings. You are always doing something to bless me. You have blessed me in so many ways that I cannot begin to count them. So how can I repay You? I can give You money - to repay You for all that You have given to me.

I know it pleases You when I give back to You with a joyful heart. However, I know money is just the beginning. What brings You true delight is my obedience to Your Word. You have given me the capability of hearing and obeying You, so seeing me act on what You tell me brings You great satisfaction. Therefore, Lord, I choose to obey You. Write it in Your book, because I find great joy in obeying You. I read Your book and listen to Your Spirit so I will know what You want me to do.

You know that I like to talk about You. I tell everyone how wonderful You are. I am always ready to tell anyone who will listen about Your great salvation and Your steadfast love. Now I have even more to tell them, since once again, You have delivered me from a very bad situation.

Please do not stop looking after me! It seems so easy for me to get into trouble. Evil temptations appear everywhere I look. You know how easily tempted I am in some areas. So, please keep on delivering

*Changing Me, Change the World*

12 For evils have encompassed me beyond number; my iniquities have overtaken me, and I cannot see; they are more than the hairs of my head; my heart fails me.

13 Be pleased, O Lord, to deliver me! O Lord, make haste to help me!

14 Let those be put to shame and disappointed altogether who seek to snatch away my life; let those be turned back and brought to dishonor who desire my hurt!

15 Let those be appalled because of their shame who say to me, "Aha, Aha!"

16 But may all who seek you rejoice and be glad in you; may those who love your salvation say continually, "Great is the Lord!"

17 As for me, I am poor and needy, but the Lord takes thought for me. You are my help and my deliverer; do not delay, O my God!

me while You teach me how to resist temptation. Deliver me while I am resisting the evil ones who want to destroy my life. Let them be desolate from their failure to separate me from Your fellowship.

Let Your people rejoice with me. I will share with them how You are my deliverance. Then we will all proclaim, "Let the Lord be magnified!"

Lord, I know that I will not ever outgrow my need for You to take care of me. You are - and will always be - my Help and my Deliverer. Keep me in Your thoughts and work out Your plans in my life. And maybe next time, Lord, would You deliver me a little more quickly?

# Psalm 41

1 Blessed is the one who considers the poor! In the day of trouble the Lord delivers him;

2 the Lord protects him and keeps him alive; he is called blessed in the land; you do not give him up to the will of his enemies.

3 The Lord sustains him on his sickbed; in his illness you restore him to full health.

4 As for me, I said, "O Lord, be gracious to me; heal me, for I have sinned against you!"

5 My enemies say of me in malice, "When will he die and his name perish?"

6 And when one comes to see me, he utters empty words, while his heart gathers iniquity; when he goes out, he tells it abroad.

7 All who hate me whisper together about me; they imagine the worst for me.

8 They say, "A deadly thing is poured out on him; he will not rise again from where he lies."

9 Even my close friend in whom I trusted, who ate my bread, has lifted his heel against me.

10 But you, O Lord, be gracious to me, and raise me up, that I may repay them!

11 By this I know that you delight in me: my enemy will not shout in triumph over me.

12 But you have upheld me because of my integrity, and set me in your presence forever.

13 Blessed be the Lord, the God of Israel, from everlasting to everlasting!

Amen and Amen.

# The Bedfast Psalm

Here I am, Lord, flat on my back. I am so sick that I cannot even hold up my head. I have been here so long, Lord. Things look hopeless, Father, but I am *not* without hope.

I have hope because I remember Your promises. You said that You would bless those who take care of the weak and the poor; that You would deliver him in time of trouble. You promised to protect him and keep him alive, to deliver him from the will of his enemies.

You have kept those promises for me, already. I am still alive, even if I am sick. You have delivered me from my enemies. Nevertheless, here is the promise that I am holding to the tightest: (This is also the one I need the most.) You said that You would strengthen me when I was sick in bed; that You would transform my illness. I really do need that right now. I am completely helpless. I am miserable beyond words.

Beyond my physical needs, Lord, I need Your forgiveness for my sins, too. My inner self needs healing just as much as my outer one does.

This illness has gone on for what seems like forever. I know that some people are probably saying, "Well, I just wish she would die and get it over with!"

I am not so sick that I do not recognize when my visitors come to speak clichés and gather gossip to take back to their friends. I am sure they leave me, go straight to the gossip party, and imagine the worst about me. I can just hear them now,

"Isn't it terrible that she's got this horrible disease?"

"I wonder what she did for God to punish her this way."

"She's so sick that she can't even get out of bed."

"She must have done something dreadful!"

"I don't think she'll ever recover."

# My Prayer

I guess that is all I can expect, since even my best friend is tired of visiting me. I do not even get a phone call from her, anymore.

Everybody else may fail me, but You will not, Lord. I know that I can trust in You. Be merciful and gracious to me, Lord. Heal me so those busybodies will have to find someone else to gossip about. Show me Your favor and do not let this disease conquer me.

Regardless of the way You answer my prayer, Lord, I will never stop praising You. Whether I am alive in this world or have passed through the valley of the shadow of death and live in the next one, I remain in Your presence. Whether in the weakness of my illness or the strength of my recovery, I continue to praise You, my Lord and my God, from this age to the next - and forever!

Amen and amen.